A SIMPLE GUIDE TO SPSS®
for Political Science

A SIMPLE GUIDE TO SPSS®
for Political Science

LEE A. KIRKPATRICK
The College of William & Mary

QUENTIN KIDD
Christopher Newport University

WADSWORTH
CENGAGE Learning™

Australia • Brazil • Japan • Korea • Mexico • Singapore • Spain • United Kingdom • United States

A SIMPLE GUIDE TO SPSS® for Political Science

Lee A. Kirkpatrick, Quentin Kidd

Senior Publisher: Suzanne Jeans

Acquisitions Editor: Anita Devine

Development Editor: Lauren Athmer, LEAP Publishing Services, Inc.

Assistant Editor: Laura Ross

Editorial Assistant: Scott Greenan

Senior Art Director: Linda Helcher

Program Manager: Caitlin Green

Manufacturing Planner: Fola Orekoya

Permissions Account Manager, Images/Media: Jennifer Meyer Dare

Production Service and Compositor: S4 Carlisle Publishing Services

For product information and technology assistance, contact us at **Cengage Learning Customer & Sales Support, 1-800-354-9706**
For permission to use material from this text or product, submit all requests online at **www.cengage.com/permissions.**
Further permissions questions can be emailed to **permissionrequest@cengage.com**

ISBN-13: 978-1-1113-5379-7
ISBN-10: 1-1113-5379-4

International Student Edition:
ISBN-13: 978-1-1113-5380-3
ISBN-10: 1-1113-5380-8

Wadsworth
20 Channel Center Street
Boston, MA 02210
USA

Cengage Learning is a leading provider of customized learning solutions with office locations around the globe, including Singapore, the United Kingdom, Australia, Mexico, Brazil and Japan. Locate your local office at **international.cengage.com/region**

Cengage Learning products are represented in Canada by Nelson Education, Ltd.

To learn more about Delmar, visit **www.cengage.com.**
Purchase any of our products at your local college store or at our preferred online store **www.cengagebrain.com**
Instructors: Please visit login.cengage.com and log in to access instructor-specific resources.

Printed in the United States of America
1 2 3 4 5 6 7 15 14 13 12 11

Contents

PART 1 How to Use IBM SPSS Statistics   **1**

Chapter 1

Introduction to IBM SPSS Statistics   **3**

Starting SPSS   4

Working with the Data Editor   5

Entering the Data   6

Naming the Variables   7

Specifying the Analysis   9

Viewing the Results (Output)   11

Editing the Output   12

Printing the Output   12

Saving the Data Set   13

Retrieving the Data Set   14

Exiting SPSS for Windows   14

Chapter 2

More on SPSS: Data Transformations, Case Selection, and Options   **15**

Computing a New Variable from Existing Variables   15

Recoding Values of an Existing Variable   18

Selecting Cases for Analysis   20

Setting Options in SPSS   22

General Options   23

Output Label Options   24

Chapter 3

The ANES 2008 Data Set   **26**

Downloading and Opening the Data File in SPSS   27

Understanding the Data Set   28

PART 2 Procedures 34

Chapter 4

Frequency Distributions and Descriptive Statistics 36
Sample Problem 36
Statistical Analysis 37
Running the Analysis in SPSS 38
Output 41
Conclusion 45

Chapter 5

Making Simple Comparisons and Controlled Comparisons 46
Sample Problem 46
Statistical Analysis 46
Running the Analysis in SPSS 47
Output 53
Conclusion 56

Chapter 6

Chi-Square Test of Significance 57
Sample Problem 57
Statistical Analysis 57
Running the Analysis in SPSS 58
Output 61
Conclusion 63

Chapter 7

One-Sample *t*-Test 65
Sample Problem 65
Statistical Analysis 65
Running the Analysis in SPSS 66
Output 66
Conclusion 68

Chapter 8

Independent-Samples *t*-Test 69
Sample Problem 69

Statistical Analysis 69
Running the Analysis in SPSS 70
Output 71
Conclusion 73

Chapter 9
Correlations **74**
Sample Problem 74
Statistical Analysis 74
Running the Analysis in SPSS 75
Output 79
Conclusion 80

Chapter 10
Simple Linear Regression **81**
Sample Problem 81
Statistical Analysis 81
Running the Analysis in SPSS 82
Output 86
Conclusion 90

Chapter 11
Multiple Linear Regression **91**
Sample Problem 91
Statistical Analysis 91
Running the Analysis in SPSS 93
Output 94
Conclusion 98

Chapter 12
Logistic Regression **99**
Sample Problem 99
Statistical Analysis 99
Running the Analysis in SPSS 101
Output 101
Conclusion 104

Chapter 13

One-Way Independent Groups ANOVA   **105**

   Sample Problem   105
   Statistical Analysis   106
   Running the Analysis in SPSS   108
   Output   112
   Conclusion   115

Chapter 14

Two-Way Independent Groups ANOVA   **116**

   Sample Problem   116
   Statistical Analysis   117
   Running the Analysis in SPSS   117
   Output   120
   Conclusion   123

Appendix: Using Syntax in SPSS   *124*

Preface

A variety of computer software options are available for use in introductory statistics and research methods courses in political science. Although programs designed specifically for teaching purposes and/or ease of use have obvious advantages, there are also good reasons to prefer a more advanced, research-oriented program such as *IBM SPSS Statistics* (*SPSS* for short). First, SPSS is in widespread use, so if one moves to another setting to finish college, pursue a graduate education, or work in an applied research setting, the odds are good that one version or another of SPSS will be available at the new location. Second, learning a powerful program such as SPSS in an introductory course prepares the student for data analysis in subsequent, more advanced courses, as well as in "real" research projects later on. It might be a little rough at first, but in the long run the extra investment of time and effort early on will pay off.

This book was written to cover what the first-time or casual user needs to know—and *only* what the user needs to know—to conduct data analyses in SPSS at the level of an introductory research methods and quantitative analysis course in political science. A small number of other books and manuals have been published with similar intentions, but we have not found one that we felt quite accomplished the goals as simply and inexpensively as we think should be possible. Some, for example, give equal coverage to one or more computer programs in addition to SPSS; a reader interested only in SPSS must sift through (and pay for!) the irrelevant pages to find what he or she needs. Other books attempt to achieve a level of comprehensiveness paralleling that of the program itself, delving into advanced multivariate techniques, complicated data transformation procedures, and so forth that are of little value to the beginning student. Still other books delve deeply into the theory and mathematics of the procedures, and consequently overlap with—and potentially conflict with—textbook material and classroom instruction. Finally, some other books are linked to a specific introductory text, thus requiring their use as a package (and often an expensive one at that). In contrast, our

ix

approach is to create a simple anthology of examples to illustrate the kinds of analyses typically covered in an introductory research methods course in political science, providing just enough explanation of procedures and outputs to permit students to map this material onto their classroom and textbook knowledge, but still leaving plenty of room for instructors to develop topics as they choose.

SPSS uses an interface we refer to as the *Point-and-Click* method that eliminates the need to learn any syntax or command language. Rather than typing commands into the program, as was required in the earliest versions of SPSS, the user merely point-and-clicks his or her way through a series of windows and dialog boxes to specify the kind of analysis desired, the variables involved, and so forth. The program is generated internally and thus is invisible to the user. The user can then examine the output without ever viewing the program code itself—in fact, users must go out of their way to view the internally generated program code at all—and without having to ever learn any syntax or computer programming skills.

Although the simplicity of this procedure seems ideal at first, we believe it is at best a two-edged sword. *IBM SPSS Statistics* also permits the user to type commands the old-fashioned way (which we refer to as the *Syntax Method*) rather than simply pointing-and-clicking. Coverage of this method is provided in a separate appendix for ease of use. There are several good reasons for learning how to use SPSS in this way rather than relying exclusively on the Point-and-Click Method. First, we think there is pedagogical value in students' learning a little computer programming, if only at the simple level of the SPSS command language, as part of an introductory statistics or methods course. Second, for anyone planning to use SPSS for more advanced purposes than completing a few homework assignments, there is simply no escaping SPSS syntax: You will probably want to learn it sooner or later. As you move on to more sophisticated uses of the program for real research projects, the advantages of being able to write and edit command syntax increase. For example, if you mis-specify a complex analysis and want to go back and rerun it with minor changes, or if you wish to repeat an analysis multiple times with minor variations, it is often more efficient to write and edit the program code directly than to repeat point-and-click sequences. Finally, and perhaps most important, some procedures in SPSS are available only via the Syntax Method; there simply is no way to accomplish them by pointing-and-clicking. For all these reasons, we have included in the appendix the Syntax-Method commands corresponding to the analyses presented in each chapter. Thus, beginning users and course instructors can choose to focus on one or the other method—or both, in parallel or sequentially.

For our sample problems, we use the American National Election Studies (ANES) database, as it is well-known and widely used in most research areas of Political Science. An introductory chapter will provide an overview of this data base and describe a variety of variables available for analysis to be used in subsequent chapters, along with relevant internet links and screen shots. Each subsequent chapter will begin by describing a research problem to be addressed, along with a discussion about the variable(s) to be analyzed in that chapter and the statistical analyses to be employed. The remainder of the chapter will present a step-by-step discussion of the analysis, and the final section will present and discuss the results of the analysis.

This book is designed primarily to serve as an inexpensive companion volume to any standard introductory research methods text in political science, and for use in such a course. The types of analyses covered, as well as their sequence of presentation, are designed to parallel the sequence of topics covered in a typical introductory research methods course in political science. However, the book should prove useful not only in other courses, but to first-time -users of SPSS in many other contexts as well.

We would like to thank the following reviewers of the manuscript for heir helpful suggestions: Brandon Bartels (George Washington University); Wesley Hussey (Sacramento State University); Paul Kellstedt (Texas A&M University); and William Wilkerson (SUNY Oneonta).

Lee A. Kirkpatrick

Quentin Kidd

About the Authors

Lee A. Kirkpatrick is professor of psychology at the College of - William & Mary in Williamsburg, Virginia. He received his B.S. from Lynch-burg College, his M.A. in general/experimental psychology from the University of Texas at El Paso, and his Ph.D. in social/personality psychology from the University of Denver. For more information, visit his home page at *http://faculty.wm.edu/lakirk.*

Quentin Kidd is associate professor of political science and chair of the Government Department at Christopher Newport University in Newport News, Virginia. He received his B.A. and M.A. from the University of Arkansas and his Ph.D. from Texas Tech University. His research interests include civic participation, survey research, and southern politics. For more information visit his home page at *www.quentinkidd.com.*

PART 1

How to Use IBM SPSS Statistics

IBM SPSS Statistics, like earlier versions of SPSS, is designed to be a comprehensive data analysis package for use in research and business. (Hereafter, we will refer to the program *IBM SPSS Statistics* simply as *SPSS* for short.) As such, it is designed to do many things, which means that there is a lot to learn in order to use it.

This book has been divided into two parts. In Part 1, which all users should read, we explain the general ins and outs of using SPSS—from entering (or importing) data, to specifying the desired analysis, to examining and manipulating the program's output (results). These basic steps are a part of any kind of analysis, so users must understand them before they proceed to the second part of the book.

Chapter 1 presents an overview of the entire process of entering and analyzing data in SPSS, from start to finish. Chapter 2 then adds a selection of more advanced topics that are also crucial for effective use of the second half of the book, such as data transformations and setting options within SPSS. In Chapter 3, we introduce a "real" political-science data set and provide instructions for downloading it from the internet and getting into a form that will be most useful for the remainder of the book.

With these essential building blocks in place, Part 2 of the book then presents details for conducting a variety of specific forms of statistical analysis most common to political science research.

Chapter 1

Introduction to IBM SPSS Statistics

The statistical analysis computer program that is the subject of this book, currently known as *IBM SPSS Statistics*, has a long history. It was first developed in 1968 by a political scientist and two computer scientists to analyze surveys, and it was originally named *Statistical Package for the Social Sciences*. The name was later shortened to simply *SPSS*.

A few decades ago, before the advent of personal computers, SPSS was one of a small number of statistical analysis programs designed to run on "mainframe" computers. In those days, a single large computer, located in a central site on a college campus or institution, was shared by multiple users, who wrote programs and input data by way of (in historical order) reels of punched tape, stacks of punched cards, or workstations with monitors and keyboards. When the personal computer came onto the scene in the 1980s, SPSS and other competitors developed versions of their programs with the capability to run on these. Although the programs made statistical analysis much easier than writing one's own computer programs from scratch, they still required users to learn their own proprietary computer languages to enter data and specify analyses; one had to type the data into a computer file in a particular format, and then type out the appropriate commands (which, of course, had to be learned) to be executed by the SPSS program in order to read the data correctly and execute the desired analysis.

Later still, a new interface emerged in the world of personal computers that involved using a pointing device, such as a mouse, as an alternative to typing commands. Users could now simply "point" to menu options and "click" on them to execute commands. SPSS quickly adapted to this new environment and its program made statistical analysis easier than ever by allowing users to enter data directly into a spreadsheet-like interface, before then specifying desired analyses by pointing-and-clicking their way through menus. This general form of the program has been around now for roughly 15 years.

Although the name and ownership of the program have changed a bit over that time, the newest version—the name of which reflects the acquisition of SPSS, Inc. by the IBM Corporation—continues to work in that same way. Today, *IBM SPSS Statistics* is one of the most widely used statistical analysis programs in the world and is very commonly used by political scientists and other social science researchers. Because of its widespread use, it is important to learn how to use the program to analyze data from political science research.

With this background and history in mind, we now turn to an overview of the program and outline the basic procedures for (1) creating a data set, (2) specifying statistical analyses; and (3) examining and manipulating your output. Once you get the hang of the program from this chapter, you will be ready to learn a few more advanced things about it in Chapter 2, and then be ready to start analyzing the data from a "real" political-science data set as described in Chapter 3 and beyond.

Starting SPSS

The SPSS program is started in different ways depending on the installation. Typically, the program is started from Windows by simply double-clicking on the appropriate icon or by choosing it from a menu of options. After the program is finished "loading," your screen should look like Figure 1.1. If SPSS opens in a small window rather than filling the entire screen, click on the maximize button in the far upper-right corner to enlarge it.

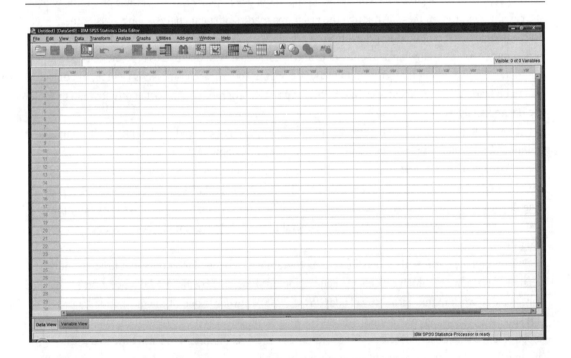

Figure 1.1 Data Editor window after first starting SPSS

Do not be surprised if, when SPSS first starts up, the screen shown in Figure 1.1 is partially obscured by a small window asking "What do you want to do?" and listing several options. If this happens, click **Cancel** to get rid of this. Your screen should now look like Figure 1.1.

A Quick Tour of the Screen

When you first start the program, the window in the foreground (or, alternatively, the only window visible on the screen) is the *Data Editor*. At the very top is a program title ("Untitled—IBM SPSS Statistics Data Editor"), as well as *minimize*, *restore*, and *close* buttons. (If this window does not occupy the entire screen, a *maximize* button will appear instead of *restore*.)

The second line, which contains the (clickable) words **File**, **Edit**, and so on, is called the *menu bar*. Clicking on any of these words produces a pull-down menu of options from which to choose in order to accomplish certain tasks. We use several of these pull-down menus in this book.

The third line, containing a row of icons, is known as the *tool bar*. These buttons provide shortcuts for tasks otherwise accomplished via the pull-down menus. For example, the button with the printer on it does the same thing as choosing **File**, then **Print**, from the menu bar. The particular buttons appearing on the tool bar can vary widely, depending on the personal computer in use. The functions of these buttons are not necessarily self-evident from the picture icons, but you can find out what a particular button does by resting the cursor (using the mouse) on top of it but not clicking on it. When you rest the cursor on one of these buttons, a brief phrase appears summarizing the button's function. We do not use the tool bar much in this manual, but you might want to experiment with it on your own.

Working with the Data Editor

When you first open the SPSS program, the Data Editor contains no data, of course—it is up to you to provide the data to be analyzed. Throughout this book we will base all of our data-analysis examples on an existing data set that you will learn about in Chapter 3. Because that data set is very large and complex, however, it will be easier for you to become accustomed to using SPSS by first learning how to create your own (small) data set from scratch.

The Data Editor functions much like a spreadsheet program. Data are stored in a matrix in which rows represent individuals or respondents (or whatever entities were measured) and columns represent different variables (that is, things about those entities that have been measured). The point at which each row and each column intersect is called a *cell*, so if you have 20 respondents (rows) and 10 variables (columns), you have 200 cells, each containing one bit of data (or *datum*). Initially, of course, the cells are all empty. Later in this chapter we describe how to add your own data into this spreadsheet and in Chapter 3 we explain how to import an existing data set into this matrix.

In this manual we deal with numerical data only—that is, data composed solely of numbers. For various reasons, even categorical variables such as sex (male, female) or party identification (Republican, Democrat, Independent) are best "coded" (assigned) as numbers rather than as letters or words. The most obvious system for coding categories of a variable is simply to assign the numbers 1, 2, 3, and so on to the categories.

With this in mind, imagine that you have asked five classmates to complete a brief survey on which they are asked to report their sex, age, and political party preference (with the choices *Republican*, *Democrat*, and *Other*). For sex, we will use the number 1 to represent males and the number 2 for females; for political party affiliation, we will use the number 1 for Republicans, the number 2 for Democrats, and the number 3 for Others. Compiled into a list, your results might look like this:

Sex	Age	Party
1	19	2
2	21	2
1	18	1
2	18	3
2	20	1

Next, we discuss how to enter these data into SPSS, run a simple statistical analysis, and examine your results.

Entering the Data

Entering the data into the Data Editor works just as you would expect. Click in the first cell of the first row and type the number **1** to represent the first student's sex. Now click on the next cell to the right and enter **19** (the first student's age), and then click on the next cell to the right to enter a **2** (the first student's party preference). Alternatively, you can use the arrow keys on your keyboard to move from cell to cell. Once the first row of data are entered, start in the leftmost cell of the second row to enter the next student's data, and so on until all five rows of data have been entered. After typing the very last value, in the third column of row 5, either hit the **Enter** key or click in another cell somewhere to store that last bit of data. The screen should now look like Figure 1.2.

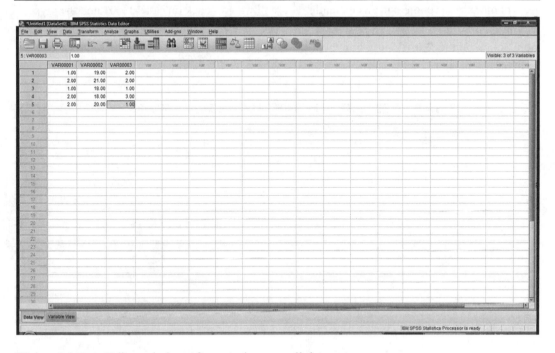

Figure 1.2 Data Editor window after entering a small data set

You will have noticed that as soon as you enter a number into a column for the first time, SPSS automatically fills in a title at the top of the column. It has assigned names to your variables. Of course, SPSS has no idea what these numbers represent, so it assigns names such as "VAR00001," "VAR00002," and "VAR00003." This is fine for SPSS, but it is not very convenient if you have to remember that, for example, "VAR00001" represents gender. You will probably want to change these names to something more meaningful.

Naming the Variables

To rename the variables, click on the tab labeled **Variable View** at the lower-left corner of the screen to produce a window that looks like Figure 1.3. (You probably did not realize it, but you were previously looking at the so-called *Data View*). In the first column of the table is the list of variable names assigned by SPSS. The remaining columns include other information about each variable that we can ignore for now, but to which we will return in a subsequent chapter. To change each name, simply click in the cell containing the existing variable name and type in the new name of your choice. In this example, you will want to click on **VAR00001** and then type **Sex** in its place; then replace **VAR00002** with **Age**, and **VAR00003** with **Party**. When you are done, click on the **Data View** tab in the lower-left corner of the screen to return to the screen containing the actual data values.

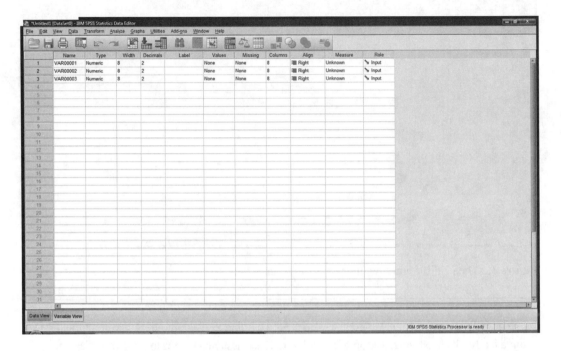

Figure 1.3 'Variable View' in Data Editor

Note that we have chosen variable names that are words or abbreviations that will help you to remember what the variables represent. For example, *gender* or *sex* is obviously a good name for a variable that distinguishes men from women. It makes no difference to the program's capability itself what the variables are named. The important thing is that you assign each of your variables a distinct name and that you remember what these names represent. In the present example, the names *Sex*, *Age*, and *Party* are good choices.

Specifying the Analysis

Once you have your data in the Data Editor—whether you entered it yourself (as you did earlier) or retrieved an existing data set, such as the ANES 2008 data (discussed in the next chapter), you are ready to tell SPSS what you would like it to do with those data—that is, what kind of statistical analysis you wish to conduct. There are basically two ways of accomplishing this, although in this book we discuss what is by far the most common method used in undergraduate political science classes: what we refer to as the *Point-and-Click Method*. (The alternative method, which we refer to as the *Syntax Method*, is far less commonly used in undergraduate classes and so we summarize it in the Appendix.)

To specify a desired analysis in SPSS, you usually begin by clicking on **Analyze** on the menu bar at the top of the screen, which produces a pull-down menu listing various categories of statistical procedures from which to choose. Choosing any of these options by clicking on it typically produces yet another menu of options, and so forth, until you reach the particular kind of analysis you wish to do. Once you have found and clicked on the name of the analysis you desire, a *dialog box* appears in which you specify the details for the analysis you have selected, such as the names of the variables to be used in the analysis and various other options. (In Part 2 of this book we explain these details for running various kinds of analyses of interest to political science researchers.) Once you have made all of your choices within a dialog box, you will eventually click on the button labeled **OK** and SPSS will spring into action. That is all there is to it.

For our current example, let us simply request *frequency distributions* for each of our three variables. We will discuss this topic in detail in Chapter 4; for now we just want to get a general sense of how to run a statistical analysis in SPSS. To request this analysis, click on **Analyze** on the menu bar at the top of the screen. This produces a pull-down menu containing a variety of options, such as **Compare Means and Correlate**. From this menu, click on **Descriptive Statistics**. This produces yet another menu containing items such as **Frequencies…**, **Descriptives…**, and **Explore…**. From these, choose **Frequencies…** to specify that you want frequency distributions. This produces a dialog box on your screen, on top of the other windows, that looks like Figure 1.4. (Do not worry if your dialog box looks a little different than our illustration; for example, the order in which the names of your variables are listed on the left-hand side of the box might be different than shown here. We will take up that issue in Chapter 2.)

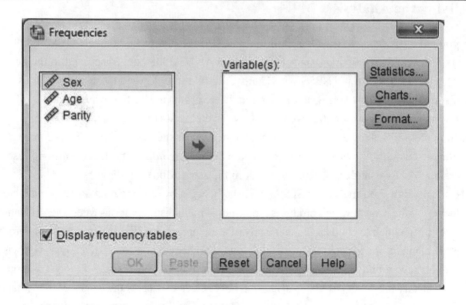

Figure 1.4 Dialog box for Frequencies analysis

Most of the dialog boxes for specifying procedures in SPSS for Windows are similar to this dialog box in several respects. On the left is a box containing the names of all of the variables that currently exist in your data set. To the right is another (empty) box labeled "Variable(s)." The goal is to move from the left box to the right box the names of the variable(s) for which you want frequency distributions. Do this by clicking on one of the variable names to highlight it, and then clicking on the right-arrow button between the boxes to move it. The variable name disappears from the left box and appears in the right box. (Alternatively, you can just double-click on a variable name and it will move to the other box immediately.) Simply repeat this procedure for each variable desired—in this case, all three. If you make a mistake or change your mind, you can single-click on a variable in the right-hand box, and then click on the middle arrow (which will have switched to a left-pointing arrow when you clicked on the variable name) to remove it from the "Variable(s)" list. For now we will ignore all of the other buttons in the dialog box—we will come back to them in Chapter 4, so just click on **OK** now to run the analysis.

Viewing the Results (Output)

Once you have run the analysis, the output produced by SPSS appears in a new window called the *Output Viewer*. This window contains the results of your analysis, and in this example should look something like Figure 1.5. (This window may appear in front of your previous screen in a reduced size; if so, click the maximize button in the upper-right corner of this window to produce the full-screen view shown in Figure 1.5.) On the left side of the screen is an outline (a table of contents, so to speak) listing the sections of your output; to the right (and taking up most of the screen) is the output itself.

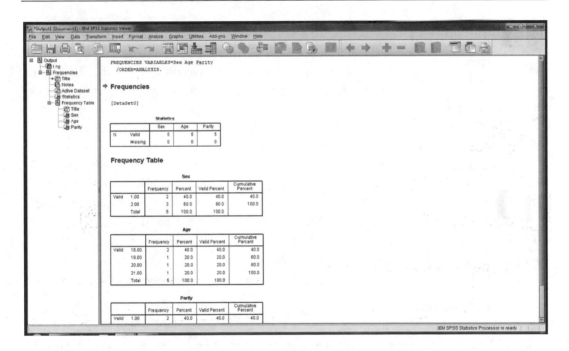

Figure 1.5 Output Viewer window with results of Frequencies analysis

Obviously, the first thing you want to do is examine the results of your analysis. You can move around within the window using the arrow keys on the keyboard, or use the mouse to manipulate the scroll bars along the window's right and bottom edges. For a different view, try clicking on **File** on the menu bar at the top of the screen, then click on **Print Preview** from the pull-down menu. This gives you a full-screen view of an entire page of output, just as it would appear if you printed it.

Experiment with the **Zoom In** and **Zoom Out** buttons on this new screen to change the view to a size you like, and with the **Next Page** and **Prev Page** buttons if the output comprises more than one page. Scroll bars appear on the right and/or bottom edges of the screen when you need them. To return to the main Output Viewer screen (Figure 1.5) at any time, click on **Close**.

In Chapter 4, we will discuss the results of the Frequencies command in detail, so do not worry now about the results that SPSS produced. Note that the first table tells us that for each of our three variables, there are five "Valid" values and zero "Missing" values (an issue we will discuss further in Chapter 3), and that the second table—labeled "Sex"—shows that our data contain two respondents whose sex was coded as 1 and three whose sex was coded as 2.

Editing the Output

Before saving and/or printing the output file, you might want to modify it somewhat. Editing the contents of the Output Viewer window seems very complicated to us, so for beginning users we recommend not doing much editing of output files.

The one editing task that is relatively simple, and often desirable, is deleting sections of unwanted output. In many procedures, SPSS prints out tables of information that you do not really need, so you might want to delete these sections to save paper and unclutter your printout. This is where the outline on the left side of the Output Viewer window comes into play. If you click on an item in that outline—say, **Title** or **Log**—two things happen: (1) the word you clicked on is selected (and appears highlighted) and (2) the specified section of the output appears in the large window (if it did not already) surrounded by a box identifying what is in that section. You can delete this entire section by simply hitting the *Delete* key on the keyboard.

Printing the Output

Printing the contents of the output window is simple. From the main Output Viewer window (Figure 1.5), click on **File** on the menu bar and choose **Print** from the pull-down menu. A dialog box appears somewhere on your screen. First, be sure the box labeled "Copies" contains the number of copies you want printed (usually **1**). Then choose between "All visible output" and "Selection" by clicking on the circle to the immediate left of the one you choose. "All visible output" means to print everything displayed in the output window: This is probably the one you want. If you want to print only part of the output, we recommend editing the output in SPSS (see the preceding section) to remove the unwanted portions, and then printing "All visible output." You can also print from the **Print Preview** window by simply clicking on the **Print** button at the top of this screen, and then following the instructions just given.

Saving the Data Set

Once you have created a data set and (re)named your variables, you will want to save it for future use. While the data editor is on your screen, click on **File** in the menu bar near the top of the screen, then click on **Save** from the resulting drop-down menu. A dialog box will appear as illustrated in Figure 1.6. Use the controls at the top of the dialog box to navigate to the folder where you want to save the file; then, change the "File name" to whatever you wish to call it, and click the **Save** button to finish the job. By default, SPSS will automatically append ".sav" to the end of the file name you provide: This means that the file is stored in the format we want, namely an SPSS data file. So, for example, if you type in the file name **MySurvey**, the name of the file on your computer will be "MySurvey.sav."

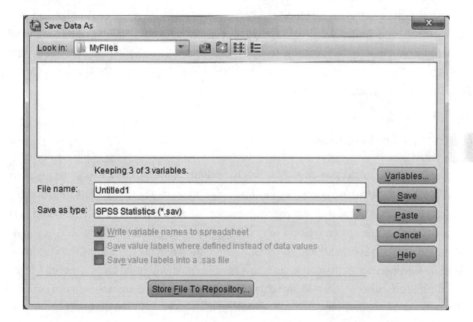

Figure 1.6 Dialog box for saving data set under a new name

Retrieving the Data Set

Of course, the point of saving the data set is so you can retrieve it on a subsequent occasion to use again. Opening an existing data file is very much like the process of saving one, as described above. After starting up SPSS, begin by clicking on **File** on the menu bar, but this time choose **Open** from the pull-down menu. This will open yet another menu of options, the first of which is *Data*. Clicking on **Data** will open a dialog box that is similar in most ways to the one in Figure 1.3. As you did when saving the file, use the controls at the top of the dialog box to navigate to the folder on your computer containing the file you are looking for. Once you find that location, you should see the name of the file (e.g., "MySurvey.sav"). Double-click on the file name to open the file. You will now be in the Data Editor, the contents of which should look exactly as they did when you saved the file.

In most installations there is a second (and even easier way to) open your data file and start up SPSS at the same time. In *Windows Explorer* or *My Computer*, open the folder containing the data file and just double-click on the file name (e.g., **MySurvey.sav**). Assuming the computer you are using knows that ".sav" files are associated with SPSS, this will open the SPSS program and your data file simultaneously, and you will be ready..

Exiting SPSS for Windows

Once you are finished analyzing your data and reviewing your output, you will be ready to exit SPSS for Windows. This can be done in various ways. One way is to choose **File** from the menu bar and then **Exit** from the pull-down menu. Another is to click the *close* button in the very upper-right corner of the screen (the button with the ¥ on it). If you have not saved your work, you will be prompted about whether you wish to save the contents of each of the windows (data, output, and perhaps syntax) that are currently open. If you have already saved these items before exiting there is no need to do so again. If you forgot to save something, you can click on **Cancel** when asked about saving one of these files, then go back to the appropriate window and save it properly before exiting.

Chapter 2

More on SPSS: Data Transformations, Case Selection, and Options

Now that you have had an overview of the basics of SPSS, this chapter introduces a few more advanced topics that will be important to know about in subsequent chapters.

In the simple data analysis example used in Chapter 1, all of your data were entered into SPSS in ready-to-use form. There are many situations, however, in which you might wish to create new variables from existing ones, or to change the values of existing variables after the data have been entered. As we will see in subsequent chapters, such *data transformations* are often required to modify or create variables in ways that enable us to run appropriate statistical analyses to answer our questions about the data. The first several sections of this chapter explain how to use SPSS to do the most common kinds of data transformations you will need to do.

The last section of the chapter will be particularly important once you begin to do the analyses discussed in subsequent chapters, which are based on the data set described in Chapter 3. In this section we explain how to set some critical options in SPSS to ensure that, in those later chapters, what you see while using SPSS matches our descriptions and illustrations. Please be sure to read this section carefully and follow the instructions provided before moving on to subsequent chapters.

Computing a New Variable from Existing Variables

One kind of data transformation involves creating a new variable based on a mathematical formula involving your original variables. For example, your data might include responses to five survey items that you wish to add up to construct a "total" score. Although you could do these computations yourself and then enter the *total* variable into the Data Editor, there are many advantages to entering the original five variables into the Data Editor and then letting SPSS create the *total* variable for you. Not only is this likely to be faster, but SPSS will not make any arithmetic errors.

Suppose you have data on five variables (or questions) that are named *q1, q2, q3, q4,* and *q5*. Now you want to create a new variable named *total*, which, for each respondent, represents the sum of his or her responses to the five questions. After opening your data into the Data Editor, click on **Transform** on the menu bar, and then choose **Compute Variable . . . .** This produces a

15

large dialog box, as illustrated in Figure 2.1, that contains a list of your variables (in this case, those in the ANES data set) on the left; blank sections labeled "Target Variable" and "Numeric Expression" at the top; and a section resembling a calculator in the middle.

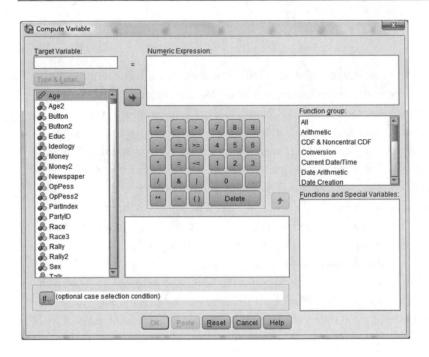

Figure 2.1 Dialog box for computing a new variable from existing variables

To create the new variable, first click in the box labeled "Target Variable" and type the word **total** (or whatever you wish to name the new variable). Then click in the box to the right labeled "Numeric Expression," and type an algebraic formula indicating how this variable is to be computed. For this example, you would type **q1 + q2 + q3 + q4 + q5**. Alternatively, you might want to compute the new variable as the average of the five variables rather than the sum by typing **(q1 + q2 + q3 + q4 + q5)/5**. After typing the desired equation, click on **OK** and you are finished. If you go back and look at the Data Editor, you will see that a new column called "total" has been added at the end. You might want to compute a few of these *total* scores by hand to confirm SPSS's computations.

Another way to construct your equation is by selecting (clicking on) the equation components, one by one, from the various parts of the window. For example, after typing **total** into the "Target Variable" box, you can create your equation by first clicking on **q1** in the variable list on the left; then, click on the arrow button next to this list and **q1** will appear in the "Numeric Expression" box as if you had just typed it yourself. Next, click on + in the calculator section of the window, and + appears after **q1** in the "Numeric Expression" box. You can construct the entire equation this way, step by step, though this is more tedious than simply typing out the equation.

In general, arithmetic operations are specified using + for addition (as in the example above), − for subtraction,* for multiplication, and / for division. SPSS understands the standard rules of algebra for sequence of operations (for example, multiplication and division before addition and subtraction), and parentheses can be used where needed or for clarification. Note that you may insert extra spaces anywhere in the command (as above) to enhance readability, but this is not necessary. In addition, a variety of more complex mathematical functions is available for use in writing equations. You can find them listed in the box under the words "Function group." For example, **sum(q1,q2,q3,q4,q5)** and **mean(q1,q2,q3,q4,q5)** are alternative formulas for the *total* variable in our earlier examples. With a little experimentation you should be able to figure many of these out and how to use them.

Conditional Computations

Sometimes you want to compute a new variable for only certain respondents, or by using a different formula for different respondents, depending on their scores on other variable(s). Such "conditional computations" are also easy to do in SPSS.

Suppose that you have another variable in your data set called *group*, and you want to compute *total* as described above only for respondents in group 1 (that is, only for respondents who have a value of 1 on the variable *group*). Follow the preceding steps, but instead of clicking on **OK**, click on the button labeled **If . . .** (which appears above the **OK** button). This produces a new (but similar) dialog box in which you specify the condition that must be met in order for the computation to be carried out. First, click in the little circle next to the phrase "Include if case satisfies condition." Then click in the box directly below this phrase, and type an equation specifying the selection criterion. In this case, the formula is simply **group = 1**. Now click on **Continue** to return to the main "Compute Variable" dialog box, and then click on **OK** to execute the instructions. If you were to go back to the Data Editor, you would see that the new variable *total* appears in the last column, but only some of your subjects (those in group 1) have a value on this variable. All others simply have a dot (indicating a "missing value") for the variable *total*.

Alternatively, use any of the following in place of the equals sign within parentheses: < or **LT** for "less than," > or **GT** for "greater than," <= or **LE** for "less than or equal to," or >= or **GE** for "greater than or equal to." **EQ** can also be used in place of =.

If you wish, you can now compute values for *total* for other respondents using an alternative formula. For example, *total* may be computed as the sum of questions 6 through 10 (instead of 1 through 5) for respondents in group 2. Simply follow the steps just described, substituting the new expressions as appropriate. When you click on **OK**, SPSS will present a pop-up warning box asking if you want to "Change existing variable?" This is because the variable you are creating (*total*) already exists—you created it in the previous step when computing scores for group 1. Now you are modifying an existing variable rather than creating a new one; you are changing "missing" scores for group 2 subjects (which is what they were after the first step) to the computed values you want. So, simply click **OK.** It is still a good idea, however, to pause for a moment to make sure you have not made a mistake. It is always dangerous to change the values of an existing variable because, in some cases, it is difficult to undo the change if you later realize you made an error.

Recoding Values of an Existing Variable

Another common data transformation involves changing the numerical codes assigned to different values of a variable, a process called *recoding* a variable. For example, suppose that for the variable *sex,* men are coded 1 and women are coded 0, but for some reason you decide that you need men to be coded 2 and women to be coded 1. Once the data have been loaded into the Data Editor, you can easily have SPSS recode these values, or change some or all of the values to entirely new values (for example, change all of the 0s to 7s and all the 1s to 28s).

It is dangerous to alter the data for an existing variable. If you make a mistake, it might be difficult to undo the change and correct the original data. Fortunately, it is very easy to save the results of the recoding as a new variable with its own name, leaving the original variable unchanged. After we explain the basic procedure for recoding a variable, we will explain how to do so by creating a new variable while leaving the original variable unchanged. In general we recommend the latter procedure to be on the safe side.

After opening the data into the Data Editor, click on **Transform** on the menu bar, and then choose **Recode into Same Variables . . . .** The resulting dialog box, shown in Figure 2.2, contains a list of your variables on the left. Move the variable(s) you want to recode from the left box to the right box (labeled "Variables"), and then click on **Old and New Values . . . .**

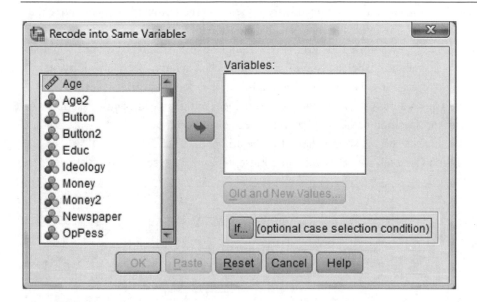

Figure 2.2 Dialog box for recoding the values of an existing variable

In the next dialog box you will see (not shown here) that there are several ways to specify the recoding; we discuss the simplest one here. In the left column under "Old Value" and next to the word "Value," type the first value of the variable you wish to change. If, as in our previous example, you wanted to change all the 0s to 1s, type **0** in this box. Then click in the box to the right, under "New Value," and type the value you want—in this case **1**. Next, click on the button labeled **Add**, just below your new value. A box in the lower right of the screen shows the results of your transformation. It now says "0 → 1." The other boxes will be blank, and you can repeat the steps for any other values you wish to recode. To complete this example, type **1** in the "Old Value" box and **2** in the "New Value" box, then click on **Add** again, and finally click on **Continue** when you are finished. Back at the main "Recode" dialog box, click on **OK** to execute the changes. The data in the Data Editor are now changed accordingly and will appear just as if you had originally entered 1s and 2s.

Creating a New Variable

We recommend that you save the modified variable under a new name and leave the original variable unchanged. To do this, click on **Transform** on the menu bar and then choose **Recode into Different Variables . . .** from the resulting menu. This brings up a dialog box, shown in Figure 2.3, that is similar to the one discussed in the preceding section, but with one extra feature. Choose the variable you wish to recode from the list in the left-hand box, and move it to the right-hand box. Now, however, you must specify the name of the new variable you wish to create (that will contain the modified values). On the right side of the dialog box, under "Output Variable," there is a small box labeled "Name"; click in this box and type the name of the new variable you wish to create. In this example, you might call the modified variable **sex2**. Then click on **Old and New Values . . .** , and follow the remainder of the procedure just described. A new variable with the specified name (*sex2*) will be created (and can be seen in the Data Editor), in which the men have 2s and the women have 1s. The original *sex* variable will still be there, unchanged, and both variables are now available for use in future analyses.

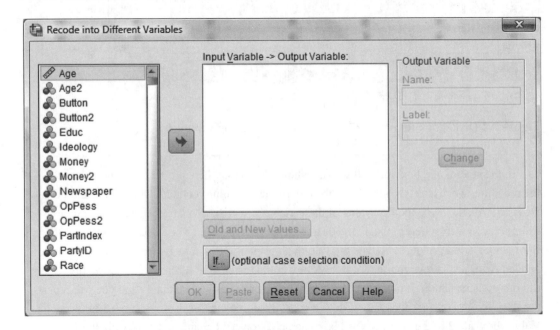

Figure 2.3 Dialog box for recoding the values of an existing variable into a new variable

Selecting Cases for Analysis

This section explains briefly how to select a subset of respondents for inclusion in one or more analyses. For example, you might want to compute a set of correlations among several variables, but you want to do so separately for men and for women. If you have a variable (for example, *sex*) in your data set to define the subgroup of interest, this is easy to accomplish without actually having to delete unwanted cases from your data.

From the menu bar, click on **Data** and choose **Select Cases . . .** in the pull down menu. This produces a dialog box (see Figure 2.4) containing a list of your variables on the left and several options from which to choose on the right. In the list on the right, notice that "All cases" is selected. Click on the circle to the left of "If condition is satisfied," and then click on the **If . . .** button below. This opens a new dialog box that looks rather similar to another one described earlier in this chapter (Figure 2.1). In the upper-right box, type an equation representing the condition that must be met for a subject to be included in subsequent analyses.

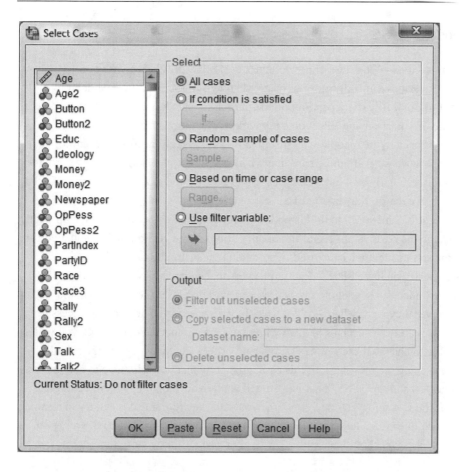

Figure 2.4 Dialog box for selecting a subset of respondents for analysis

For example, type **sex = 1** to select only men (if men have a value of 1 on the variable *sex*), or type **total < 15** to select only individuals whose score on the variable *total* is less than 15. (See the section earlier in this chapter, entitled *Conditional Computations*, for more details on specifying conditions.) Then click on **Continue** to return to the main "Select Cases" dialog box, and click on **OK** to put the selection criterion into operation. Any analyses specified subsequently will include only those subjects who have been selected. If, later in your SPSS session, you wish to conduct analyses including all of your subjects, you can turn off the selection criterion by again choosing **Data**, then **Select Cases . . .** , from the menu bar, then choose "All cases" in the dialog box.

Setting Options in SPSS

In order to accommodate a wide range of user preferences, SPSS provides a variety of options that control the way various kinds of information are displayed on the screen. The default settings for these options will vary depending on the particular installation of SPSS that you are using: For example, if you are using SPSS on a network, these options have been set in whatever way was chosen by the people who installed it. This poses a bit of a problem for us in writing this book, because we want to be sure that when you follow the instructions we provide in any given chapter, you will see what we expect you to see. We have no way of knowing what these settings are, however, on the version of SPSS you are using.

The most straightforward solution to this problem (at least, the best we could come up with!) is to have you change the settings of several important options in the version of SPSS that you are using, to match the settings that we have used in producing the instructions and illustrations throughout this book. If you have SPSS on your own personal computer, you should be able to set these options just once; subsequently, every time you start up SPSS, the options should remain set to whatever they were when you last used the program. If you are sharing access to SPSS, however, over a network such as in a lab with many interconnected computers, you will probably not be able to change these settings permanently (because then your changes would affect everyone else using the program). In this case, it is likely that you will have to change these settings every time you start up SPSS. That is, you will want to develop the habit of setting the options in SPSS as the first thing you do every time you start the program. We will try to remind you to do this in each of the chapters throughout the book. If at any time you are not seeing on your screen what we say you should be seeing, the likely reason is that your options are not set to match ours.

Next, we explain how to set those options that will be important whenever you are using this book.

General Options

On the menu bar at the top of the screen, click on **Edit** (the second item from the left), and then click on **Options...** at the bottom of the resulting menu. This will produce a dialog box that looks more or less like Figure 2.5. (Some of the selected options might be different than in our figure, of course—that is why we are here.) Across the top of the window are tabs labeled "General," "Viewer," "Data," and so on, with the "General" tab already selected. If the **General** tab is not already selected, click on it to select it.

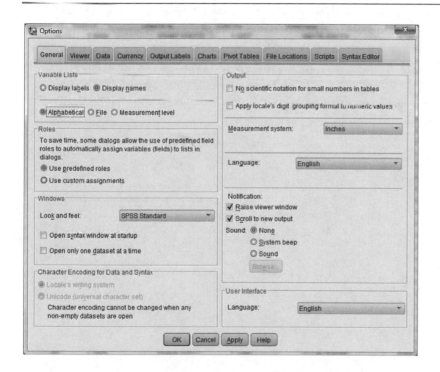

Figure 2.5 Dialog box for setting 'general' options in SPSS

In this window there are only two particular settings we are concerned about, and they are both in the upper-left corner under the label "Variable Lists." In the first row under this label, you want to select (if it is not already selected) the option *Display names* (rather than "Display labels") by clicking in the little circle next to this phrase. Then, in the next line down, you want to select (if it is not already selected) the option *Alphabetical* (rather than "File" or "Measurement level"). The window should now look just like Figure 2.5. Now click on the **Apply** button at the bottom of the screen to put these changes into effect.

Output Label Options

Next, click on the tab at the top of the window labeled **Output Labels** (the fifth tab from the left). This will produce a window that looks like Figure 2.6, though again perhaps with different options selected. In the upper-left box on this screen, under the title "Outline Labeling," we want to set the option on the first line ("Variables in item labels shown as:") to *Names*, and we want to set the option on the line below this ("Variable values in item labels shown as:") to *Values and Labels*. Then, in the lower-left box, titled "Pivot Table Labeling," we want to do the same thing as we did above. That is, we want the first option ("Variables in labels shown as:") to be set as *Names* and the second option ("Variable values in labels shown as:") as *Values and Labels*. In the end, your screen should look exactly like Figure 2.6. Now click on **OK** to put your changes into effect and exit the Options dialog box.

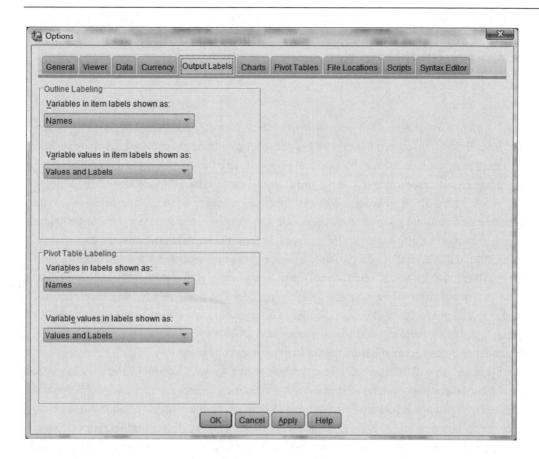

Figure 2.6 Dialog box for setting 'output label' options in SPSS

At some point in the future, once you become more familiar with SPSS, you might want to explore some of the other options available in SPSS, but these are the only settings you need to worry about now.

Remember, you will want to check these settings every time you start up SPSS, and change them again if necessary, to ensure that what you see when using SPSS matches our examples and illustrations in this book.

Chapter 3

The ANES 2008 Data Set

Although you can use this book to learn how to analyze data of your own—that is, that you have entered into SPSS as discussed in Chapter 1—our examples throughout Part 2 involve analyzing an existing, "real" data set created by political science researchers. While it is not uncommon for political science researchers to collect and code their own data, it is far more common for them to work with existing data sets. When it comes to political and social questions—the types of questions that political science researchers often address—there happens to be a large amount of data collected on a daily basis to address them. Much of these data are collected and organized into data sets and made available to researchers in political science and other fields.

These data typically are collected at one of two levels of analysis: *aggregate* or *individual*. For instance, data about cities, states, or nations, such as per capita income, literacy rates, percentage of national budgets spent on the military, and crime rates, are measured at the aggregate (group) level of analysis. Data about individual people such as age, race, level of education, voting behavior, and views about policy issues, are measured at the individual level of analysis.

In this book, we will use examples from the American National Election Studies (ANES), which is one of the most common sources of data available to political science researchers. ANES was established by the National Science Foundation in 1977 in an effort to provide a national research resource for social scientists studying elections. It built upon a survey data collection project that had taken place at the University of Michigan since 1952. Since it began, nearly 6000 academic papers based on analyses of the ANES data have been written. Because ANES is federally funded, the data are available at no charge to anyone interested in using it for research.

ANES data mostly focuses on eight general topics, although over its lifetime many different topics have been explored. The most common general topics of study have been (1) how and why people do or do not vote, (2) people's evaluations of congressional candidates, (3) people's evaluations of presidential candidates, (4) how and to what degree people are involved and participate in politics, (5) people's commitment to and trust in the political system, (6) people's views on public policy issues, (7) people's ideology and partisanship, and (8) people's social and religious characteristics. The questions included in the ANES are developed by a board of academic experts from across the country, and unlike most survey studies, ANES surveys are conducted in person by trained interviewers. The examples and illustrations in this guide all come from the *ANES 2008 Time Series Study*, a study conducted around the 2008 presidential election, including preelection and postelection interviews with people.

In this chapter, we explain how to retrieve the set from the Internet and bring it into SPSS, give you a quick tour of the data, and provide instructions for making some changes to the data in SPSS to make it easier to work with in subsequent chapters.

Downloading and Opening the Data File in SPSS

The full versions of all of the ANES data sets, including the 2008 Time Series Study, are available on the Internet at **http://www.electionstudies.org/**.

In this book, however, we utilize only a particular version of this data file, which has been placed on a different web site available for download, for several reasons. First, the data set available for download at the web site listed above is updated regularly which creates the possibility that the version of the data set you download might differ somewhat from the version that was used to prepare this book. Second, the original data set is very large, containing over 2,000 variables, only a handful of which are used in the examples in this book. It therefore made sense to provide you with a version of the data set that is faster to download and easier to navigate. Third, the variables in the original data set are named in ways that are not at all intuitive, making it difficult to figure out which variable measures what. In the modified version of the data set we are making available to you, the variables have been renamed in a much more user-friendly manner (which we explain later in this chapter). We hope that these changes will make the data set much easier for you to use, so that you can focus on learning how to analyze the data in SPSS with minimal distraction and confusion.

This modified version of the *ANES 2008 Time Series Study* data file used throughout this book can be downloaded at:

http://www.cengage.com/politicalscience/kirkpatrick/SPSSforpoliticalscience1e.

At this site, just click on the link labeled **Download Data** to download the file. Be sure to remember where (i.e., in which folder on your computer) you saved it! The name of the file should be *ANES2008-ASimpleGuideToSPSSForPoliticalScience.sav*.

Now, open the SPSS program, as discussed in Chapter 1. Near the top of the page (which should look like Figure 1.1 back in Chapter 1) you'll see a row of clickable links (the *menu bar*) labeled as **File**, **Edit**, **View**, and so on. Follow the instructions from Chapter 1, in the section labeled *Retrieving the Data Set*, to open the file. That is, click on **File** to produce a drop-down menu with numerous options; then click on **Open** in this list to reveal another menu of four options; and from this menu, choose **Data...**. This will produce a dialog box similar to Figure 3.1. (Notice that this is the same procedure discussed in Chapter 1 for opening any previously saved data set, in the section entitled "Retrieving the Data Set.")

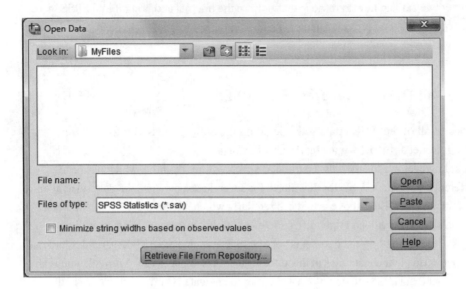

Figure 3.1 Dialog box for opening an existing data set

Use the controls at the top of this dialog box to navigate to the folder containing the file that you downloaded (*ANES2008-ASimpleGuideToSPSSForPoliticalScience.sav*). Once you find the folder, double-click on the file name (or, click once on the filename to highlight it, then click the **Open** button) and SPSS will whir into action.

Understanding the Data Set

Once the ANES 2008 data have loaded into the SPSS program, your *Data Editor* screen should look like Figure 3.2.

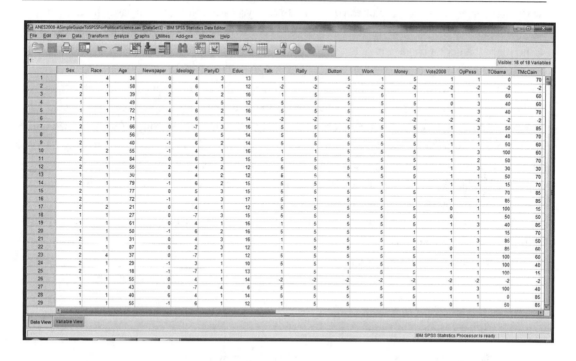

Figure 3.2 Data Editor after opening the ANES 2008 data set

In this textbook we deal with numerical data only—that is, data composed solely of numbers. The particular variables used include basic demographic information such as sex, age, race, education, region of country, ideology, and party identification. We also use variables about behavior such as presidential vote choice and how much attention was given to news about the presidential campaign. Variables tapping into opinions about policy questions such as attitudes toward gay marriage and laws to protect gays and lesbians from discrimination, attitudes toward abortion, attitudes about illegal immigration as well as views about whether illegal immigrants should have a path to citizenship, and a general measure of optimism are used. Finally, several variables called "feeling thermometers" that measure feelings about public figures including George W. Bush, Barack Obama, John McCain, Hillary Clinton, and Sarah Palin are included.

Variable Names

When entering data into SPSS, unique names must be assigned to each variable so that they can be referred to later when specifying the analysis you want. In the original data set, the names that ANES has assigned to variables are not very informative. The variable representing respondents' sex or gender, for example, is named *v081101*. (In case you are curious, this is partly because in earlier versions of SPSS, prior to version 12.0 of SPSS for Windows, variable names were restricted to no more than eight characters in length, partly because it is very difficult to come up with meaningful-sounding names for over 2,000 variables given this restriction. The names of the variables that we will be using in this book have been changed to names that are more user-friendly and more easily remembered when you want to use them in data analyses. For example, *Gender* or *Sex* is obviously a good name for a variable that distinguishes men from women (we happened to choose *Sex*), and will certainly be easier to remember than the ANES-assigned name for this variable as noted above. It really makes no difference to SPSS; as far as the program is concerned, you could just as well call this variable *cabbage* or leave it as *v081101*. For us human users, however, simple descriptive names are usually much preferred.

Next is the list of the variables in this data set (with the names we have given them) along with a brief description of each one:

Sex—respondent's gender

Race—respondent's race

Age—respondent's age

Newspaper—days past week read daily online newspaper

Ideology—respondent's liberal-conservative self-placement seven-point scale

PartyID—respondent's party identification

Educ—respondent's education

Talk—did respondent talk to anyone about voting

Rally—did respondent attend political meetings, rallies, speeches…

Button—did respondent wear campaign button or post sign…

Work—did respondent do any work for party or candidate

Money—did respondent contribute money…

Vote2008—did respondent vote in 2008 election

OpPess—respondent optimistic or pessimistic about future

TObama—feeling thermometer Barack Obama

TMcCain—feeling thermometer John McCain

TPalin—feeling thermometer Sarah Palin

Tgaylesbian—feeling thermometer Gay Men and Lesbians

Another way to view the names of the variables, as well as to see additional information about them, is to click on the tab in the lower-left corner of the data screen labeled **Variable View**. (The default "view" of the data set, as shown in Figure 3.2, is the "Data View.") This produces a screen such as that illustrated in Figure 3.3. Here, you can see all of the variable names listed in the left-hand column, with additional columns providing other useful information about the variables as discussed below. We introduced this "Variable View" briefly in Chapter 1, but at that time ignored most of the information that it provides. Now that we are using the ANES data, it will be useful to understand some of this other kind of information as well.

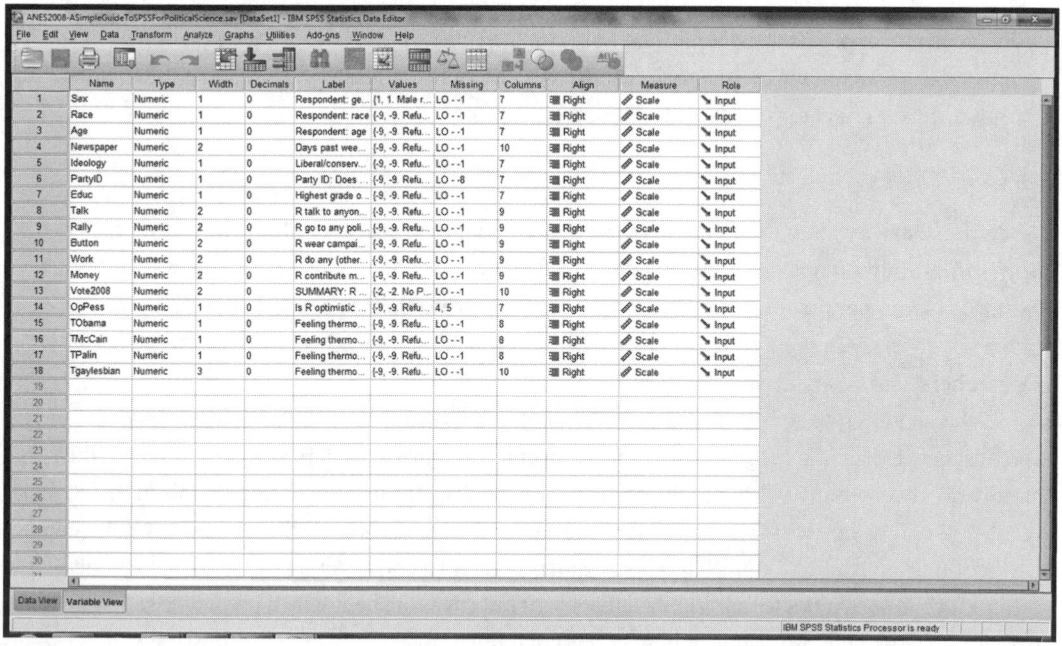

	Name	Type	Width	Decimals	Label	Values	Missing	Columns	Align	Measure	Role
1	Sex	Numeric	1	0	Respondent: ge...	{1, 1. Male r...	LO - -1	7	Right	Scale	Input
2	Race	Numeric	1	0	Respondent: race	{-9, -9. Refu...	LO - -1	7	Right	Scale	Input
3	Age	Numeric	1	0	Respondent: age	{-9, -9. Refu...	LO - -1	7	Right	Scale	Input
4	Newspaper	Numeric	2	0	Days past wee...	{-9, -9. Refu...	LO - -1	10	Right	Scale	Input
5	Ideology	Numeric	1	0	Liberal/conserv...	{-9, -9. Refu...	LO - -1	7	Right	Scale	Input
6	PartyID	Numeric	1	0	Party ID: Does ...	{-9, -9. Refu...	LO - -8	7	Right	Scale	Input
7	Educ	Numeric	1	0	Highest grade o...	{-9, -9. Refu...	LO - -1	7	Right	Scale	Input
8	Talk	Numeric	2	0	R talk to anyon...	{-9, -9. Refu...	LO - -1	9	Right	Scale	Input
9	Rally	Numeric	2	0	R go to any poli...	{-9, -9. Refu...	LO - -1	9	Right	Scale	Input
10	Button	Numeric	2	0	R wear campai...	{-9, -9. Refu...	LO - -1	9	Right	Scale	Input
11	Work	Numeric	2	0	R do any (other...	{-9, -9. Refu...	LO - -1	9	Right	Scale	Input
12	Money	Numeric	2	0	R contribute m...	{-9, -9. Refu...	LO - -1	9	Right	Scale	Input
13	Vote2008	Numeric	2	0	SUMMARY: R ...	{-2, -2. No P...	LO - -1	10	Right	Scale	Input
14	OpPess	Numeric	1	0	Is R optimistic ...	{-9, -9. Refu...	4, 5	7	Right	Scale	Input
15	TObama	Numeric	1	0	Feeling thermo...	{-9, -9. Refu...	LO - -1	8	Right	Scale	Input
16	TMcCain	Numeric	1	0	Feeling thermo...	{-9, -9. Refu...	LO - -1	8	Right	Scale	Input
17	TPalin	Numeric	1	0	Feeling thermo...	{-9, -9. Refu...	LO - -1	8	Right	Scale	Input
18	Tgaylesbian	Numeric	3	0	Feeling thermo...	{-9, -9. Refu...	LO - -1	10	Right	Scale	Input

Figure 3.3 'Variable View' in Data Editor containing the ANES 2008 data set

Labels and Values

In this "Variable View" (shown in Figure 3.3), the column titled "Label" contains a more detailed description of what each variable represents (i.e., beyond its short name). Because these labels are generally too long to fit in the default screen display, you need to expand the width of that column to be able to read most of them. Do this by floating your cursor over the word "Label" at the top of the column, and then slowly moving it to the right, toward the top of the next column ("Values" in this case). When the cursor is positioned right over the boundary between the two cells, it will turn into a double-headed arrow. When this happens, left-click and drag the double-headed arrow toward the right. This will move the column boundary to the right, making the contents of the now-wider column visible.

The next column to the right, labeled "Values," contains information about which numbers were assigned to which responses. We noted above, for example, that in the ANES 2008 data, the variable representing respondent's gender (named *Sex*) is coded such that 1s represent males and 2s represent females. To confirm this, find the row for variable *Sex* (row 1), move your cursor over to the cell in the column titled "Label," and click near the right-hand side of the cell (i.e., over the "..."). This produces a dialog box containing the labels assigned to each value of the variable. If you wanted to change these labels or assign additional labels, you would do that here by typing the value and label in the appropriate places at the top of the box, and then clicking on **OK**. We are not, however, interested in changing these—we will just use the descriptions that ANES has already provided—so for now, click **Cancel** to get rid of the dialog box.

Missing Values

As in most survey studies, ANES respondents do not always answer all of the questions. Sometimes they do not know the answer to a question, or they choose not to answer it. For example, some people might not feel comfortable sharing their age or income with an interviewer, or even their political party affiliation. Such nonresponses are referred to by researchers as *missing data*.

When entering data from the survey into a computer (using either SPSS or some other spreadsheet or database program), some researchers simply leave such missing data blank—they simply do not enter any value into the corresponding cell of the data set. If you do this in SPSS, the blank cell will be automatically converted into a period which is how SPSS represents what it calls "system-missing values." ANES and many other researchers, however, prefer to assign a variety of different codes or values to missing data that carry information about why a particular variable, for a particular respondent, is missing. These codes are referred to as "user-assigned missing values." Numbers are assigned to represent these various missing-value categories, taking care to assign numbers that could not possibly represent valid responses. For instance, the value of -9

(i.e., "minus 9") might be assigned if a respondent refused to answer, whereas the value of −8 might be assigned if a respondent did not know the answer. If valid answers to this question are all numbers between 1 and 9, for example, we can safely use −8 or −9 to represent missing values without confusing real data with missing data. It is important to make sure, however, that SPSS knows that these numbers represent categories of missing data rather than real data values. For example, if we were asking SPSS to compute the mean of the scores on a variable whose valid scores range between 1 and 9, we would want SPSS to exclude those respondents who have been assigned missing values in doing its calculations, rather than averaging those −8s and −9s together with the valid scores.

Fortunately, as with variable labels and values, ANES has already taken care of this in our data set. If you have already looked at the "values" assigned to a variable for which multiple missing-values codes were assigned, as discussed above, you will have seen the descriptions for these codes. (Note that for the *Sex* variable mentioned above, no special descriptions were listed for missing codes.) To see the missing-value codes that were assigned to a given variable, click near the right-hand edge of the cell in the column labeled "Missing." In some cases there might be discrete values coded as missing, such as −8 or −9; in other cases an entire range of values is assigned as missing. (For the gender variable *Sex*, all values from "LO" to "−1" are assigned as missing values—that is, any number equal to less than −1. Sometimes it is just easier for the user, as a practical matter, to assign such a range of missing values than to list multiple discrete values.)

PART 2

Procedures

The preceding chapters provided an overview of the various steps involved in conducting data analysis in SPSS, from data entry to output, while also introducing the ANES 2008 data set that we will use throughout the remainder of the book.

In Part 2, we fill in the details for a variety of statistical procedures commonly used by political science researchers. For each type of analysis, the book (1) presents a sample problem, (2) provides a brief overview of the statistical analysis appropriate for answering the research question posed in the sample problem, (3) shows how to conduct the analysis in SPSS, (4) explains the output produced by the procedure, and finally (5) summarizes the conclusion to be drawn about the research question in the sample problem.

Chapter 4

Frequency Distributions and Descriptive Statistics

Sample Problem

At the beginning of the semester you were intrigued to hear one of your classmates describe how shocked he was when Barack Obama won the election in 2008 because he had assumed that, on average, Americans were pretty conservative and liked Sarah Palin a great deal. You have thought about his assumptions on and off since then, and now that you are at a point in the semester at which you are able to work with data, you want to investigate those assumptions of his.

The ANES 2008 has over 2,000 respondents and the values assigned to the variables *Ideology* and *TPalin* for the first 30 respondents are listed here so we can get a better understanding of the data.

Respondent	Ideology	TPalin
1	4	70
2	6	−2
3	6	70
4	4	70
5	6	70
6	6	−2
7	−7	70
8	6	85
9	6	85
10	4	50
11	6	85
12	4	60
13	4	85
14	6	85
15	5	70
16	4	70
17	4	50
18	−7	50
19	4	85
20	6	85
21	4	65
22	2	40
23	−7	60
24	3	0
25	−7	0

26	4	−2
27	−7	40
28	4	85
29	6	85
30	4	50

As we can see by examining the *Variable View* screen in the Data Editor, respondent number 1's score of 4 on *Ideology* means "moderate; middle of the road" and is the midpoint of the 1–7 scale, while rating Sarah Palin a 70 on the feeling thermometer that ranges from 0 to 100. Respondent number 2 is "conservative" (a score of 6) in terms of ideology and has a missing value on the feeling thermometer question for Sarah Palin. Respondent number 24 is "slightly liberal" (a score of 3) and rates Sarah Palin a 0 on the feeling thermometer. Instead of examining each individual case like this, however, you will want a summary view of the whole sample. To get that, you want to construct frequency distributions and obtain some basic descriptive statistics for these two variables.

Statistical Analysis

The term *Descriptive Statistics* refers broadly to various ways of summarizing data using tables, graphs, and numbers (the latter being referred to as "statistics"). In this chapter we demonstrate how to obtain all of these in SPSS.

The *frequency distribution* of a variable refers to a table or graph that shows, for each possible value or score, how many respondents had that particular value or score. For example, a frequency distribution for the variable *Ideology* will show us how many people answered with a 1 ("extremely liberal") how many with a 2 ("liberal") and so forth, all the way up to 7 ("extremely conservative"). In table form, a frequency distribution will contain a column listing all of the different values observed in the data (for *Ideology*, 1 through 7) and for each, the *frequency* of that value (i.e., how many respondents had that value). Such a table typically also includes additional columns that report these frequencies as a *percentage* or *proportion* of the total sample (known also as *relative frequencies*) and/or as *cumulative frequencies*—that is, for any given value, the number (or percentage or proportion) of respondents who had a score or value either equal to or less than that value.

Because such tables can be quite large for some variables, it is often easier to "see" a variable's distribution by converting it from tabular to graphical form. Two common types of graphs for frequency distributions are *bar charts* and *histograms*. A bar chart is just like a frequency table, except that the frequency for each value is displayed visually as a "bar," the height of which reflects the number of respondents with that value or score. A bar chart will work well for our *Ideology* variable. A histogram works the same way except that it first groups scores into (equal-sized) intervals, which is particularly useful when there is a very large number of different scores. For our variable *TPalin*, it will be useful to use a histogram in which scores are grouped into a smaller number of intervals, such as 5–10, 15–20, and so on.

When summarizing data with numbers, these numbers are referred to simply as "statistics." Commonly used statistics include various kinds of averages, including the *mean* (the simple arithmetic average, computed by adding up all the scores and dividing by the number of scores), the *median* (the score that half of the respondents are below and half above), and the *mode* (the most common scores, i.e., the score with the largest frequency.) Other important statistics include various measures that reflect the variability of the scores, including the *variance* and the *standard deviation* (the latter being the square root of the former), and a measure for determining how bunched up on one side of a distribution or the other the distribution is, called *skewness*.

Running the Analysis in SPSS

Open SPSS and retrieve the ANES 2008 data file described in Chapter 3. Then, be sure to set SPSS *options* per our instructions in Chapter 2.

To begin, click on **Analyze** on the menu bar. This produces a pull-down menu containing a variety of options, such as **Compare Means**, **Correlate**, and so on. Now click on **Descriptive Statistics**. This produces yet another menu containing items such as **Frequencies…**, **Descriptives…**, and **Explore…**. Choose **Frequencies…**to specify that you want frequency distributions. This produces a dialog box somewhere on your screen, on top of the other windows, that looks like Figure 4.1.

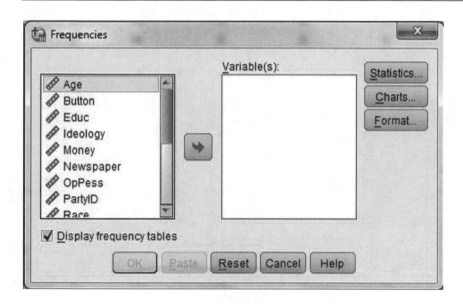

Figure 4.1 Main dialog box for Frequencies analysis

Many of the dialog boxes for specifying procedures in SPSS for Windows are similar to this dialog box in several respects. On the left is a box containing the names of all of the variables. To the right is another (empty) box labeled "Variable(s)." The goal is to move from the left box to the right box the names of the variable(s) for which you want frequency distributions. Do this by clicking on one of the variable names to highlight it, and then clicking on the right-arrow button between the boxes to move it. The variable name disappears from the left box and appears in the right box. (Alternatively, you can just double-click on the variable name and it will move to the other box immediately.) Simply repeat this procedure for each variable desired. If you make a mistake or change your mind, you can single-click on a variable in the right-hand box, and then click on the middle arrow (which will have switched to a left-pointing arrow when you clicked on the variable name) to remove it from the "Variable(s)" list. In this example, we want to choose **Ideology** and **TPalin**, the two variables of interest.

You may now click on **OK** to run the analysis. However, if you would like to have SPSS print out descriptive statistics or graphs in addition to the frequency distribution, do not click on **OK** yet but instead keep reading.

Descriptive Statistics

To the right of this dialog box, you will see three other buttons labeled **Statistics…**, **Charts…**, and **Format…**. If you wish to obtain descriptive statistics along with your frequency table, click on **Statistics…** to produce a new dialog box, as illustrated in Figure 4.2.

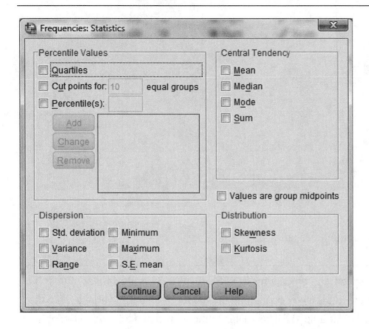

Figure 4.2 Dialog box for specifying descriptive statistics in Frequencies analysis

Apart from the section labeled "Percentile Values" and the line "Values are group midpoints," the remaining sections of the box list a variety of descriptive statistics. Simply click on the little box to the left of each statistic you wish SPSS to calculate for you; a check mark will appear in each selected box. (Note that if you wish to unselect a box you have already selected, simply click on it again.) The sample output shown later in this chapter is the result of requesting the *Mean*, *Median*, and *Mode* boxes under "Central Tendency," the *Skewness* box under "Distribution," and the *Std. deviation* box under "Dispersion." When finished, click on **Continue** to return to the previous dialog box (Figure 4.1). Click on **OK** to run the analysis, or follow the instructions in the next section to obtain a graphical frequency distribution as well.

Histograms and Bar Graphs

To obtain histograms or bar charts in addition to frequency tables (and/or descriptive statistics), click on **Charts…** at the right in the dialog box illustrated in Figure 4.1 to produce a new dialog box as illustrated in Figure 4.3. Initially, SPSS assumes you do not want any graphs ("charts")—the little circle next to "None" is selected by default. Click on the circle next to "Bar chart" or "Histogram" to indicate the kind of frequency distribution graph you prefer. (Later in this chapter we illustrate the output produced by requesting a histogram for the variable *TPalin* and a bar char for *Ideology*.) Then click **Continue** to return to the previous dialog box (Figure 4.1), and click on **OK** to run the analysis.

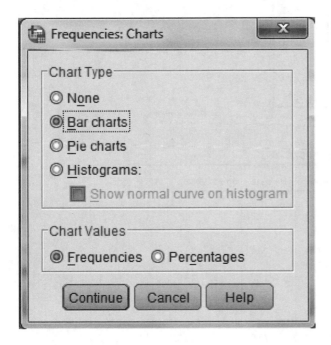

Figure 4.3 Dialog box for specifying graphs in Frequencies analysis

Output

Selected parts of the output produced by SPSS for the sample problem are illustrated in Figure 4.4. SPSS first displays a table of descriptive statistics for all of the specified variables, followed by frequency distributions for each variable separately.

Frequencies

Statistics

		Ideology	TPalin
N	Valid	1626	1982
	Missing	697	341
Mean		4.14	48.33
Median		4.00	50.00
Mode		4	50
Std. Deviation		1.542	27.033
Skewness		-.133	-.179
Std. Error of Skewness		.061	.055

Frequency Table

Ideology

		Frequency	Percent	Valid Percent	Cumulative Percent
Valid	1 1. Extremely liberal	70	3.0	4.3	4.3
	2 2. Liberal	230	9.9	14.1	18.5
	3 3. Slightly liberal	188	8.1	11.6	30.0
	4 4. Moderate; middle of the road	514	22.1	31.6	61.6
	5 5. Slightly conservative	238	10.2	14.6	76.3
	6 6. Conservative	311	13.4	19.1	95.4
	7 7. Extremely conservative	75	3.2	4.6	100.0
	Total	1626	70.0	100.0	
Missing	-9 -9. Refused	5	.2		
	-8 -8. Don't know	17	.7		
	-7 -7. Haven't thought much about it	675	29.1		
	Total	697	30.0		
Total		2323	100.0		

Figure 4.4 Output from Frequencies analysis

The table of descriptive statistics lists for each variable the number of cases that were included in the analysis ("Valid") and the number not included ("Missing"), along with the statistics described above. SPSS gives us all of the descriptive statistics we asked for, for each variable we include in our analysis.

Of course, it is up to us to know which statistics are appropriate to use and which are not appropriate to use in our analysis. In this case, Ideology is an *ordinal* variable, so the appropriate measure of central tendency to use is the *median*, which equals 4.00. The average ideology of Americans, as described using this statistic, is "moderate; middle of the road." Most of the other statistics are appropriate for use only with scale variables such as *TPalin*. The appropriate measure of central tendency to use is the *mean*, which equals 48.33 (on a scale from 0 to 100). The *standard deviation* and *skewness* statistics tell us something about the spread and shape of the distribution of the data around the mean for a scale variable. In this case, the *standard deviation* of 27.033 tells us that about 2/3 of the scores fall within 27.033 points of the mean. The skewness statistic of $-.170$ tells us that scores are slightly bunched up on the left side of the distribution (or on the end toward the low scores, in this case). We can better see this "bunching" when we look at a histogram later in the chapter.

The first column in each Frequency Table lists all values that were found on the variable; the second column ("Frequency") lists the number of cases having that value; the third column ("Percent") is the percentage of all cases having this value (that is, frequency divided by total number of cases); the fourth column ("Valid Percent") is the percentage of all "valid" cases (cases that were not missing data on this variable) having that value; and the fifth column lists the cumulative percentage for that value (the percentage of valid cases having that value or less). Note that "Percent" and "Valid Percent" would be identical if there were no missing values on the variable.

Histograms and Bar Graphs

Figure 4.5 illustrates a histogram for the variable *TPalin* and Figure 4.6 illustrates a bar chart for the variable *Ideology*, as produced by the procedures described earlier. Notice that for TPalin, SPSS has divided the range of scores into varying intervals (e.g., 5–10, 10–12, 12–15, 15–20, and so on), and the heights of the respective bars represent the frequencies of these categories rather than individual scores. Notice in Figure 4.6, however, which illustrates a bar chart for the variable *Ideology*, that SPSS does not group the scores like this; instead, each individual value is shown by a separate bar representing the frequency of that particular score (in this case, categories of ideology). For this reason, it is generally preferable to use bar charts for variables that have only a small number of possible values (especially categorical or "nominal-level" variables, such as *Sex*), and to use histograms for variables that can take on a large or infinite number of possible values (usually scale variables). Finally, notice in the histogram the bar for category 0 is higher than the next bar: That little bump up in the lowest score represents the bunching that the skewness statistics indicated.

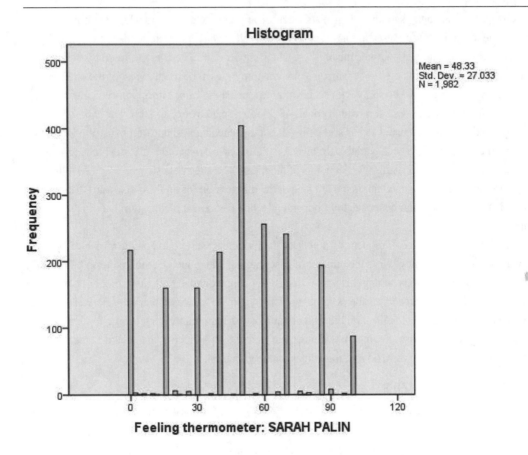

Figure 4.5 Histogram output from Frequencies analysis

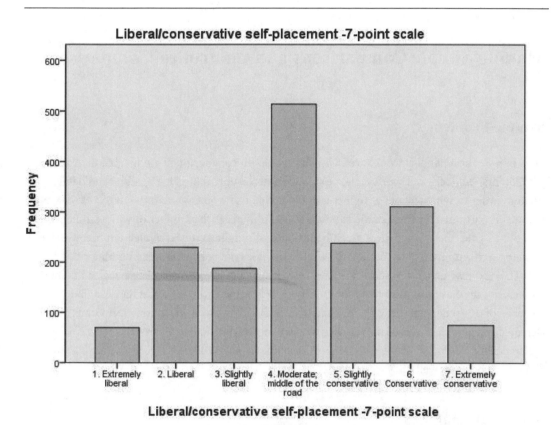

Figure 4.6 Bar Chart output from Frequencies analysis

Conclusion

The output suggests that your classmate's impression of the American public is slightly off. The median score for the variable *Ideology* was "moderate; middle of the road." Similarly, the mean of the TPalin variable—48.33 on a 0–100 scale—was very close to the middle value of the scale. It appears that on average, Americans are not "pretty conservative," as your classmate thought, and they do not, on average, "like Sarah Palin a great deal."

Chapter 5

Making Simple Comparisons and Controlled Comparisons

Sample Problem

On a pre-election panel at Rockhaven University, a political consultant claims that the "gender gap" favors Democrats. Therefore, he concludes that the only thing Democratic candidates have to do in order to win elections is to increase the number of women who turn out to vote—white women in particular. If Democratic candidates could increase the number of white women who turn out to vote, they would have much better odds of winning any given election because the gender gap is largely a phenomenon for whites and does not really exist among minorities.

The next morning in a political science research methods class, students debate the point. The professor of the class asks them to do some analysis to determine whether or not they can find evidence of a "gender gap" between men and women that shows women favoring Democrats over Republicans more than men do as well as the more complex question of whether this female preference for Democrats (if there is one) is evident only among white women or whether it is true for nonwhite women as well.

Statistical Analysis

To do this analysis, you will need to use the variables *Sex*, *PartyID*, and *Race*. Because the variables are all categorical, we will use the *cross-tabulation* function in SPSS to examine the relevant descriptive statistics in the data set and see if they appear to support the professor's hypotheses.

For the first question, the null hypothesis is that men and women do not differ with respect to party choice. The professor's alternative (research) hypothesis is that there is a difference—specifically, that the proportion of women who identify themselves as Democrats is greater than the proportion of men who do so. The cross-tabulation function in SPSS will allow us to examine the relevant proportions (or percentages) observed in the ANES 2008 data. For the second question, we will need to break down the data further by race—specifically, we want to repeat the same analysis as in the first question, but we want to do it twice, separately for white and for black respondents.

In this chapter, we examine only the descriptive statistics—the observed proportions in our sample data—to determine if they appear to be consistent with the professor's hypotheses. If we do find such evidence, however, it will be necessary to conduct a statistical hypothesis test (using the chi-square statistic) to determine if the results observed here are statistically significant and whether we can confidently rule out the possibility that our sample results might merely be the result of random sampling error. The chi-square test will be discussed in Chapter 6.

Running the Analysis in SPSS

Open SPSS and retrieve the ANES 2008 data file described in Chapter 3. Then, be sure to set SPSS *options* per our instructions in Chapter 2.

Recoding the PartyID Variable

Before we proceed with the analysis, we need to make a change to the coding of the variable *PartyID*. As it is currently configured, *PartyID* is a variable in the ANES data set with the codes:

> 1 = Democrat
>
> 2 = Republican
>
> 3 = Independent
>
> 4 = Other party (SPECIFY)
>
> 5 = No preference {VOL}.

The last two codes represent very few respondents, uncertain information about those respondents, and make the comparison that what we are going to be doing next is more difficult. The changes we want to make are rather simple. We want to keep "Democrat," "Republican," and "Independent," but remove "Other party" and "No preference." While we are at it, we are going to change the order of the three categories to follow a logical sequence, with "Independent" in the middle between the other two. Therefore, we will want to recode:

> 1 = Democrat (no change)
>
> 2 = Independent (it used to be coded 3)
>
> 3 = Republican (it used to be coded 2).

The code 4 (Other party) and 5 (No preference) will be recoded "system missing," so these respondents will not be included in the analysis at all.

To accomplish all of this, follow the instructions in Chapter 2, in the subsection entitled "Creating a New Variable" of the section titled "Recoding Values of an Existing Variable." Let us name our new variable *PartyID3* as a reminder that this is a three-category version of the *PartyID* variable. We want to recode the "old value" of 1 into the "new value" of 1 (i.e., Democrats will still be coded as 1), the "old value" of 2 into the "new value" of 3 (Republicans were coded 2, but now will be coded 3), and the "old value" of 3 into the "new value" of 2 (Independents were coded 3 but now will be coded 2).

Once you have created the new variable, go to the *Variable View* screen of the Data Editor, where you should now see a new row containing the new *PartyID3* variable. In this row, click on the cell under the column heading **Values**. When you do this, a little box will appear with three dots in it ("...)". Click on that little box to open another box called *Value Labels*, as illustrated in Figure 5.1. In the space near the top of this box labeled "Value:" type the number *1*, and then in the space labeled "Label:" type the word *Democrat*. Now, click the **Add** button to save this information. Next, follow the same procedure to create the label *Independent* (for value *2*) and *Republican* (for value *3*), and then click **OK** when you are done. You have now successfully given value labels to the variable you just recoded, which will be very helpful later for remembering which codes correspond to which values— plus, these labels will appear in the SPSS output and thus make it easier to interpret.

Figure 5.1 Dialog box for adding Value Labels in Data Editor

Before proceeding to the analyses of primary interest, it would be a good idea to examine the frequency distributions of the old and new variables to make sure you have recoded them properly. You can do this by running the *Frequencies* analysis described in Chapter 4 for both the original *PartyID* variable and your new *PartyID3* variables. Unless you have made some kind of error, you should find that the number of Democrats, Republicans, and Independents are the same for both variables. Now that we are confident that our new variable was constructed correctly, we can turn to the data analysis of interest.

One more thing—now that you have gone through the work of creating this new variable, you might want to save the revised data file (i.e., the version that includes this new variable) in case you want to use this new variable in subsequent analyses. To do so, follow the instructions in Chapter 1. You can name the new version of the data whatever you like, but we suggest something such as *ANES 2008—Revised per Chapter 5*. (We will be making other revisions to the data set in some subsequent chapters, so it might be useful for you to keep track of which revised version is which.)

Analysis 1: Simple Comparisons

To begin, click on **Analyze** on the menu bar. Now, click on **Descriptive Statistics**. So far this is a familiar territory, but now let us choose **Crosstabs . . .** to specify that you want to conduct a cross-tabulation analysis. This produces a dialog box somewhere on your screen, on top of the other windows, that looks like Figure 5.2.

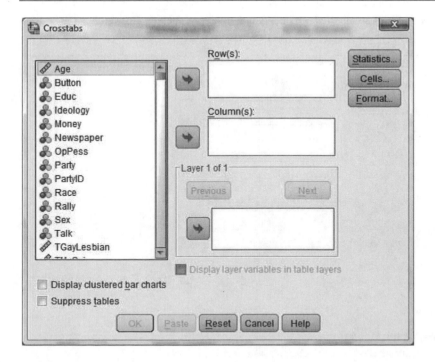

Figure 5.2 Main dialog box for Crosstabs analysis

Click on the **PartyID** variable in the list of variables in the left-hand box to highlight it, and then click on the right-arrow button between the boxes to move it into the *Row(s)* box. Because we are trying to understand the influence of gender on partisanship, *PartyID3* is our dependent variable, and dependent variables *always* go in the rows of a cross-tabulation analysis. Now, choose the **Sex** variable from the list of variables in the left-hand box to highlight it, then click on the right-arrow button between the boxes to move it into the *Column(s)* box. *Sex* is our independent variable, and independent variables *always* go in the columns of a cross-tabulation analysis.

At the upper right corner of this dialog box, you will see three buttons labeled **Statistics . . .**, **Cells . . .**, and **Format . . . .** Click on the button labeled **Cells . . .** and a smaller dialog box will open that looks like Figure 5.3. You will notice two boxes under "Count," three boxes under "Percentages," three boxes under "Residuals," and five circles under "Noninteger Weights." You only need to make sure that the "Observed" box is checked under "Counts" (which might already be done for you by default) and the "Column" box is clicked under "Percentages" (which probably has not been done for you). When conducting a cross tabulation analysis, it is important to always obtain column percentages because we read cross tabulations by examining the percentage of each category of the independent variable (in this case *Sex*) within each category of the dependent variable (in this case *PartyID3*). The remaining boxes and circles can be left as they are, so click on **Continue** at the bottom of the dialog box to return to the previous dialog box (Figure 5.2).

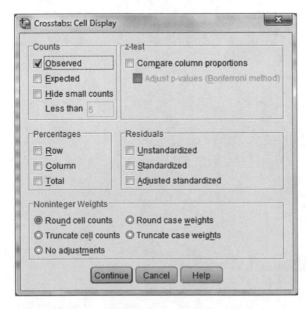

Figure 5.3 Dialog box for specifying cell-display information in Crosstabs analysis

For now, you do not need to worry about doing anything in the **Statistics . . .** button or the **Format . . .** button. (We will come back to the **Statistics . . .** button in Chapter 6.) You are now ready to click on **OK** to run the analysis.

The results from this analysis are illustrated and discussed later in this chapter. You might want to skip ahead to that section now, but do not forget to come back here to run the second analysis as explained immediately below.

Analysis 2: Controlled Comparisons

The first part of our analysis suggests that there are differences between the partisan preferences of men and women. There really is a "gender gap." But if you remember, the political consultant argued that it only existed for white women. We can carry the analysis one step further and examine whether this "gender gap" exists between white and nonwhite women by conducting the analysis again, but controlling for *Race* this time. Before we proceed, however, we will have to recode *Race* using the same procedures we just followed to create *PartyID3* in order to reduce the number of categories into which *Race* was originally coded.

The codes for *Race* in the ANES data set are:

1 = white

2 = black/African-American

3 = white and black

4 = other race

5 = white and another race

6 = black and another race

7 = white, black and another race.

The codes -9 and -4 are classified as *missing* and we will leave them that way. We want to follow the recode procedures (outlined in Chapter 2) to create a new race variable named *Race3*, just as we did earlier in this chapter to create *PartyID3*. For this new variable, we want to recode the old *Race* code 1 into a new *Race3* code 1, and the old *Race* code 2 into a new *Race3* code 2; that is, we will keep these two codes as they were. Then, however, we want to recode all of the values 3, 4, 5, 6, and 7 of the old Race variable into code 3 for the new variable Race3—that is, we want to combine all of these into a single "other" category. You can do this either by recoding one value at a time (e.g., "old value" 3 into "new value" 3, then "old value" 4 into "new value" 3, up through "old value" 7) or by using the Range function offered in the dialog box. To do this, click on the little circle next to the word "Range" on the left-hand side of the box, then type a **3** in the box immediately below the word "Range" and then a 7 in the next box down (below the word "through"). This tells SPSS that all values from 3 through 7 should be recoded the same way. Then, enter 3 for the "new value," and SPSS will make it so.

As before, make sure to go to the **Variable View** in the Data Editor and, as you did with *PartyID3*, fill in the **Values** of the new *Race3* variable. The value of 1 should be labeled "white," the value of 2 should be labeled "black/African-American," and the value of 3 should be labeled "other." This will make it much easier to read the output when you conduct your analysis. This new race variable will now be used to examine our question. Finally, as you did with the *PartyID3* variable, run a frequency analysis as described in Chapter 4 on both the *Race* and *Race3* variables to make sure you have the same number of white and black/African-American respondents. If you do, then that means you recoded properly!

Before moving on, though, you might want to re-save the data set—to include the new variable you just created—in case you want to use this new variable in subsequent analyses. To do so, follow the instructions in Chapter 1. You can name the new version of the data whatever you like, but we will use the name *ANES 2008—Revised per Chapter 5*. (If you saved your data under this particular name earlier in the chapter, SPSS will ask you if you want to replace the previously saved version with this new version; in this case, go ahead and say "yes." Alternatively, you can say "no" and provide another new name for the saved data set.)

To begin, click on **Analyze** on the menu bar. Now, click on **Descriptive Statistics**. Choose **Crosstabs** as you did before to specify that you want to conduct a cross-tabulation analysis, producing the dialog box shown previously in Figure 5.2.

Click on the *PartyID3* variable in the list of variables in the left-hand box to highlight it, and then click on the right-arrow button between the boxes to move it into the *Row(s)* box. Again, because we are trying to understand the influence of gender on partisanship, *PartyID3* is our dependent variable, and dependent variables *always* go in the rows of a cross-tabulation analysis. Now, choose the *Sex* variable from the list of variables in the left-hand box to highlight it, and then click on the right-arrow button between the boxes to move it into the *Column(s)* box. *Sex* is our independent variable, and independent variables *always* go in the columns of a cross-tabulation analysis. Now, since we want to examine the effects of race on the gender gap, choose *Race3*, the new race variable we just created, from the list of variables in the left-hand box to highlight it, and then click on the right-arrow button between the boxes to move it into the box labeled "Layer 1 of 1."

If you closed SPSS since you conducted the last analysis above, you'll need to go back and reset everything in the buttons labeled **Statistics . . .**, **Cells . . .**, and **Format . . .** as per the instructions provided for the first analysis. Once you do that, you are ready to go so click on **Continue** at the bottom of the dialog box to return to the previous dialog box. You are now ready to click on **OK** to run the analysis.

Output

The important parts of the outputs produced by our two analyses are shown in Figures 5.4 and 5.5, respectively, and are discussed in order below.

Analysis 1: Simple Comparisons

The important part of the output produced by SPSS for this problem is illustrated in Figure 5.4. SPSS produces a cross-tabulation table that shows the percentages of males and females who identify themselves as (respectively) Democrat, Independent, or Republican. Remember, our null hypothesis is that there is no difference between the partisan preferences of men and women; the alternative (research) hypothesis is that women favor Democrats over Republicans more than men do.

Crosstabs

PartyID3 * Sex Crosstabulation

			Sex		Total
			1 1. Male respondent selected	2 2. Female respondent selected	
PartyID3	1.00 Democrat	Count	364	613	977
		% within Sex	39.6%	50.9%	46.0%
	2.00 Independent	Count	357	357	714
		% within Sex	38.8%	29.7%	33.6%
	3.00 Republican	Count	198	234	432
		% within Sex	21.5%	19.4%	20.3%
Total		Count	919	1204	2123
		% within Sex	100.0%	100.0%	100.0%

Figure 5.4 Output from Crosstabs analysis: simple comparison

The output suggests that there are indeed differences in partisan preferences between men and women. We can clearly see that more females identify as Democrat than do males (i.e., 50.9% vs. 39.6%). A slightly higher percentage of men identify as Republican (21.5%) than do women (19.4%), and men identify as Independent at a higher rate than do women (38.8% vs. 29.7%). It appears that we will be able to reject the null hypothesis of no sex difference in partisan preferences. Moreover, the pattern of difference appears to fit the alternative (research) hypothesis that women favor Democrats over Republicans more than men do (rather than the other way around).

Before drawing any strong conclusions about this, however, we will need to conduct a statistical hypothesis test (specifically, a chi-square test) to determine if these observed differences are greater than can reasonably be explained by chance (i.e., whether they are "statistically significant"). We explain how to conduct this test in Chapter 6.

Analysis 2: Controlled Comparisons

The output produced by our second analysis is illustrated in Figure 5.5. Just like our earlier analysis, SPSS produces a cross-tabulation table that shows the percentages of males and females who identify themselves as Democrat, Independent, and Republican, but now it does this separately within each category of race. So we can see the percentage of males and females who identify themselves with each party, as in the first analysis, but this time separately for white respondents, black/African-American respondents, and respondents who are another race. Remember, our null hypothesis is that there is no difference between the partisan preferences of women across categories of race; the alternative (research) hypothesis is that white women favor Democrats over Republicans more than nonwhite women do.

Crosstabs

PartyID3 * Sex * Race3 Crosstabulation

Race3				1 1. Male respondent selected	2 2. Female respondent selected	Total
				Sex		
1.00 white	PartyID3	1.00 Democrat	Count	149	287	436
			% within Sex	26.2%	38.7%	33.3%
		2.00 Independent	Count	239	242	481
			% within Sex	42.1%	32.7%	36.7%
		3.00 Republican	Count	180	212	392
			% within Sex	31.7%	28.6%	29.9%
	Total		Count	568	741	1309
			% within Sex	100.0%	100.0%	100.0%
2.00 black/African-American	PartyID3	1.00 Democrat	Count	161	248	409
			% within Sex	70.6%	77.3%	74.5%
		2.00 Independent	Count	62	67	129
			% within Sex	27.2%	20.9%	23.5%
		3.00 Republican	Count	5	6	11
			% within Sex	2.2%	1.9%	2.0%
	Total		Count	228	321	549
			% within Sex	100.0%	100.0%	100.0%
3.00 other	PartyID3	1.00 Democrat	Count	52	73	125
			% within Sex	43.3%	54.5%	49.2%
		2.00 Independent	Count	56	45	101
			% within Sex	46.7%	33.6%	39.8%
		3.00 Republican	Count	12	16	28
			% within Sex	10.0%	11.9%	11.0%
	Total		Count	120	134	254
			% within Sex	100.0%	100.0%	100.0%
Total	PartyID3	1.00 Democrat	Count	362	608	970
			% within Sex	39.5%	50.8%	45.9%
		2.00 Independent	Count	357	354	711
			% within Sex	39.0%	29.6%	33.7%
		3.00 Republican	Count	197	234	431
			% within Sex	21.5%	19.6%	20.4%
	Total		Count	916	1196	2112
			% within Sex	100.0%	100.0%	100.0%

Figure 5.5 Output from Crosstabs analysis: controlled comparison

The output suggests that there is a difference between the partisan preferences of white women compared to African-American women, but not much between white women and women who identify with other races. In the top section of the table, for which Race3 equals 1 ("white"), we can clearly see that white women identify as Democrats far more than do white men (i.e., 38.7% vs. 26.2%—a difference of >12 percentage points). In the second section of the table, for which Race3 equals 2 ("black/African-American"), the sex difference is somewhat smaller: Among black/ African-American respondents, women identify as Democrats slightly more than do men (i.e., 77.3% vs. 70.6%—a difference of a little less than 7 percentage points). Interestingly, the sex difference for the other-race category is similar to that for white women than, with a strong preference for Democrats over Republicans (54.5% vs. 43.3%).

Conclusion

It appears that we will be able to reject the null hypothesis that there is no difference in partisan preferences: Women clearly favor Democrats over Republicans overall. Moreover, in the second analysis, we could see that this "gender gap" is evident within each of our three race categories considered separately. In addition, our second analysis showed, consistent with the second research hypothesis, that this gender gap appears larger among whites than among black/African-Americans.

Chapter 6

Chi-Square Test of Significance

Sample Problem

A political science student interning on a congressional campaign keeps hearing the candidate for whom she is interning claim that conservatives are more optimistic about their future than are liberals. She decides to put the claim to a test using the new statistical analysis skills she has been acquiring in her political science research methods class. The ANES includes *Ideology*, which measures political ideology ranging from very conservative to very liberal and *OpPess*, which measures whether a person is optimistic about their future, pessimistic about it, or neither optimistic or pessimistic.

Statistical Analysis

In this problem, we are testing the null hypothesis that political ideology and optimism are independent—in other words, that there is no relationship between political ideology and whether a person is optimistic or pessimistic. The alternative (research) hypothesis is that conservative political ideology and optimism are related to each other, and specifically that more conservative people are on average more optimistic.

Because both variables are categorical, the appropriate test here is the *chi-square test of independence*, sometimes called (conversely) the chi-square test of *association*, which tests the difference between the distribution in an actual sample and a hypothetical distribution based on the null hypothesis. Chi-square works by first determining what the distribution of the sample would look like if no relationship existed (the null hypothesis) and then comparing that to the distribution of the actual sample (in this case, the ANES data). If the two distributions are very similar (the sample data look just like what would be expected if the variables were unrelated to one another) the chi-square statistic will be a very small number and the result will likely not be statistically significant. If the data distribution looks very different from what would be expected by chance, however, the chi-square value will be larger and the resulting probability might allow us to reject the null in favor of the alternative (research) hypothesis.

The chi-square test, however, pays no attention to the *order* of the categories of each variable; it assumes that both variables represent only the *nominal* level of measurement, in which case it makes no sense to talk about "higher" versus "lower" scores on either variable. In our example, though, it could be argued that if both variables were coded in a certain way, so it does make sense to think about "lower" versus "higher" scores on each, they could be meaningfully regarded as *ordinal* variables. We could then ask not only whether there was any association between them at all, as chi-square is designed to do, but specifically whether respondents with higher scores on one variable (say, a more conservative ideology) tend also to have higher scores on the other variable (e.g., are more pessimistic). To think about the problem in this way, we need to ensure that both of our variables are indeed ordinal-level variables before running the analysis. In the ANES data set, the *Ideology* variable already represents an ordinal variable: Scores range from 1 ("extremely liberal") to 7 ("extremely conservative"), with intermediate values (2 through 6) representing a continuum between these extremes. We will have to recode the ANES variable *OpPess*, however, to be able to interpret it as an ordinal variable (as explained later). Then, in addition to the chi-square test discussed above, we will have SPSS compute two other statistics: *Somers' d* and *gamma*, which measure the degree to which the two variables are related to each other in this ordinal manner. In addition, each of these statistics will be accompanied by a significance test to determine whether the degree of relationship observed in the sample is strong enough that it cannot reasonably be explained by chance.

Running the Analysis in SPSS

Open SPSS and retrieve the ANES 2008 data file described in Chapter 3 (or, alternatively, the revised version of it that you created and saved in Chapter 5). Then, be sure to set SPSS *options* per our instructions in Chapter 2.

Data Transformations

Before we proceed with the analysis, we need to make a change to the coding of the variable *OpPess*. As it is currently configured, *OpPess* is a variable in the ANES data set with the codes:

>   1 = "optimistic"
>
>   2 = "pessimistic"
>
>   3 = "neither optimistic nor pessimistic."

We want to rearrange these codes so that:

>   1 = optimistic (no change)
>
>   2 = neither optimistic nor pessimistic
>
>   3 = pessimistic.

So we are simply changing the order of codes 2 and 3 so that the numbers 1 through 3 reflect an ordinal variable on which higher scores (3s) mean "more pessimistic," lower scores (1s) mean "less pessimistic" (i.e., more optimistic), and intermediate scores (2s) represent an in-between level of pessimism. To accomplish this, follow the instructions in Chapter 2 to recode the *OpPess*, as we did in creating the variables *PartyID3* and *Race3* in Chapter 5. Call the new variable *OpPess2*, and recode the values of the original *OpPess* variable as described above: That is, "old value" 1 is recoded into "new value" 1, "old value" 2 into "new value" 3, and "old value" 3 into "new value" 2.

If you wish, you can add variable labels to this new variable as we did in Chapter 5. Go to the *Variable View* screen of the Data Editor, where you should now see a new row containing the new *OpPess2* variable. In this row, click on the cell under the column heading **Values**. When you do this, a little box will appear with three dots on it ("..."). Click on that little box to open another box called *Value Labels*, as illustrated in Figure 5.1 in the previous chapter. In the space near the top of this box labeled "Value:" type the number *1*, and then in the space labeled "Label:" type the word *Optimistic*. Now click the **Add** button to save this information. Next, follow the same procedure to create the label *Neither* (for value *2*) and *Pessimistic* (for value *3*), and then click **OK** when you arere done. You have now successfully given value labels to the variable you just recoded, which will be very helpful later for remembering which codes correspond to which values—plus, these labels will appear in the SPSS output and thus make it easier to interpret.

Before going on, it is a good idea to run and examine the frequency distributions of the original and new variables to make sure you have recoded them properly, as we did in Chapter 5. Once you are sure that the new variable *OpPess2* is correct, you can proceed to the analysis.

Now that you have gone through the work of creating this new variable, you might want to save the revised data file (i.e., the version that includes this new variable) in case you want to use this new variable in subsequent analyses. To do so, follow the instructions in Chapter 1. You can name the new version of the data whatever you like, but we suggest something such as *ANES 2008—Revised per Chapter 6*.

Running the Analysis

To obtain a cross-tabulation table (as previously discussed in Chapter 5) and chi-square test of independence, click on **Analyze**, and then choose **Descriptive Statistics** from the pull-down menu. Then click on **Crosstabs . . .** to produce the dialog box illustrated in Figure 5.2 in the previous chapter.

As we saw in Chapter 5, your variable list appears in a box to the left, and you need to move the names of the variables you wish to analyze into the appropriate boxes on the right. Click on **Ideology** in the left box, then on the right-arrow button to move this variable to the box labeled "Row(s)." Then click on **OpPess2** and move it to the "Column(s)" box by clicking on the appropriate right-arrow button. (Note that the choice of row versus column variables is arbitrary in this case; you could just as easily have made *OpPess2* the row variable and *Ideology* the column variable.)

Next, click on the **Cells . . .** button at the upper right in the dialog box. This produces a new dialog box (illustrated in Figure 5.3 in the previous chapter) in which you may specify the kinds of information you would like printed in each cell of the *Ideology × OpPess2* cross-tabulation table. By default, each cell of the table contains only the number of cases for that particular cell ("Observed"). Choosing **Expected** tells SPSS to print also the expected frequencies for each cell—that is, the number of cases expected in each cell if the row variable and the column variable were independent (the "E" values in the chi-square formula). Choosing **Row** (under "Percentages") asks SPSS to print percentages relative to the number of cases per row, and choosing **Column** does likewise relative to columns. In Chapter 5 we were interested only in column percentages, but for the present analysis we have selected all of these options. Click on **Continue** when you are finished, but do not click on **OK** just yet.

There is still one more step. To request a chi-square test or other statistics, click on **Statistics . . .** at the right in the main "Crosstabs" dialog box. This produces a dialog box (see Figure 6.1) containing a list of different statistical analyses, many of which are probably unfamiliar. You may choose as many of these as you wish, but for our purposes we will select only "Chi-square" and two measures of "strength of association": *Somers' d*, and *gamma*. Then click on **Continue** to return to the main "Crosstabs" dialog box, and click on **OK** to run the analysis.

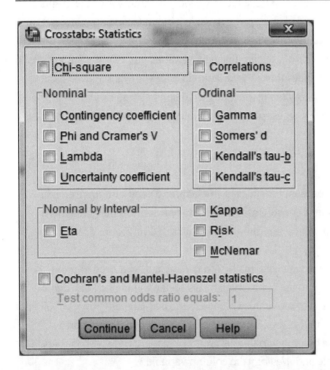

Figure 6.1 Dialog box for specifying statistics in Crosstabs analysis

Output

The important parts of the output produced by SPSS for the sample problem are shown in Figure 6.2. (The first section of the output, labeled "Case Processing Summary," is not shown.)

Crosstabs

Ideology * OpPess2 Crosstabulation

			OpPess2			
			1.00	2.00	3.00	Total
Ideology	1 1. Extremely liberal	Count	42	14	7	63
		% within Ideology	66.7%	22.2%	11.1%	100.0%
		% within OpPess2	4.2%	4.3%	5.0%	4.3%
	2 2. Liberal	Count	164	33	16	213
		% within Ideology	77.0%	15.5%	7.5%	100.0%
		% within OpPess2	16.2%	10.1%	11.5%	14.4%
	3 3. Slightly liberal	Count	124	33	12	169
		% within Ideology	73.4%	19.5%	7.1%	100.0%
		% within OpPess2	12.3%	10.1%	8.6%	11.4%
	4 4. Moderate; middle of the road	Count	299	117	48	464
		% within Ideology	64.4%	25.2%	10.3%	100.0%
		% within OpPess2	29.6%	35.7%	34.5%	31.4%
	5 5. Slightly conservative	Count	149	46	21	216
		% within Ideology	69.0%	21.3%	9.7%	100.0%
		% within OpPess2	14.7%	14.0%	15.1%	14.6%
	6 6. Conservative	Count	185	68	28	281
		% within Ideology	65.8%	24.2%	10.0%	100.0%
		% within OpPess2	18.3%	20.7%	20.1%	19.0%
	7 7. Extremely conservative	Count	48	17	7	72
		% within Ideology	66.7%	23.6%	9.7%	100.0%
		% within OpPess2	4.7%	5.2%	5.0%	4.9%
Total		Count	1011	328	139	1478
		% within Ideology	68.4%	22.2%	9.4%	100.0%
		% within OpPess2	100.0%	100.0%	100.0%	100.0%

Chi-Square Tests

	Value	df	Asymp. Sig. (2-sided)
Pearson Chi-Square	14.250[a]	12	.285
Likelihood Ratio	14.734	12	.256
Linear-by-Linear Association	3.388	1	.066
N of Valid Cases	1478		

a. 0 cells (.0%) have expected count less than 5. The minimum expected count is 5.92.

continued

Directional Measures

			Value	Asymp. Std. Error[a]	Approx. T[b]	Approx. Sig.
Ordinal by Ordinal	Somers' d	Symmetric	.045	.021	2.112	.035
		Ideology Dependent	.061	.029	2.112	.035
		OpPess2 Dependent	.036	.017	2.112	.035

a. Not assuming the null hypothesis.
b. Using the asymptotic standard error assuming the null hypothesis.

Symmetric Measures

		Value	Asymp. Std. Error[a]	Approx. T[b]	Approx. Sig.
Ordinal by Ordinal	Gamma	.076	.036	2.112	.035
N of Valid Cases		1478			

a. Not assuming the null hypothesis.
b. Using the asymptotic standard error assuming the null hypothesis.

Figure 6.2 Output fro Crosstabs analysis with statistics

The cross-tabulation table in this example includes four pieces of information for each cell, as specified in our example. A legend explaining the contents of each cell appears at the left of each row. The top number in each cell is the observed frequency ("Count"), followed below by the expected frequency ("Expected Count"), row percentage (in this case, "%within Ideology"), and column percentage ("% within OpPess2"). Thus, for example, 42 respondents were observed in the cell defined by *Ideology* = 1 and *OpPess2* = 1 (upper-left cell in the table). The expected frequency for this cell is 43.1, which could be found by hand by multiplying the number of patients in the *Ideology* = 1 row (63) by the number of respondents in the *OpPess2* = 1 column (1011) and dividing by the total number of patients in the table (1478): 63*1011/1478 = 43.094046 (which SPSS has rounded off to 43.1). This represents the number of respondents that would have been expected in this cell if the null hypothesis were true—that is, if our two variables were statistically independent of (unrelated to) one another. The row percentage ("% within Ideology") of 66.7% means that the observed frequency in this cell (42) represents 66.7% of the 63 observations in the *Ideology* = 1 row. Similarly, the column percentage ("% within OpPess2") of 4.2% indicates that the observed frequency of 42 represents 4.2% of the 1011 observations in the *OpPess2* = 1 column.

Next, several chi-square test statistics are produced, along with their associated degrees of freedom and significance levels. The chi-square statistic provides a test of the null hypothesis that the distribution of respondents across the three optimism/pessimism categories (optimistic, pessimistic, and neither optimistic nor pessimistic) is the same within each category of the Ideology variable (or, vice-versa); in other words, ideology is not related to optimism/pessimism. Of these chi-square statistics, the *Pearson* statistic is most commonly used for this purpose and is taught in most textbooks. In this case, the observed Pearson chi-square value equals 14.250, and there are 12 degrees of freedom (the product of the number of columns minus 1 and the number of rows minus 1). The associated *p*-value, labeled "Asymp. Sig. (2-sided)," is reported as .285, which means there is not a significant relationship between the two variables: The degree to which a relationship is apparent in this sample is no more than would be expected by chance.

Lastly, SPSS prints out the additional two statistics we requested for measuring the strength of the (ordinal) association between *Ideology* and *OpPess2*. Unlike the chi-square test earlier, these measures are computed based on the assumption that the two variables are both *ordinal*. In fact, we recoded one of the variables specifically so we could think of both variables in this way. (In contrast, the chi-square test is unaffected by such ordering. The results for the chi-square test would have been the same even if we had not recoded the *OpPess* variable.) The table labeled "Directional Measures" shows the value for Somers' d to be .045, which is a very small level of association. However, the associated *p*-value, labeled "Approx. Sig." is .035, which means that there is a significant association even if a very small one. The table labeled "Symmetric Measures" shows the value for gamma to be .076 and the associated *p*-value, again labeled "Approx. Sig." is .035, again suggesting a very small but statistically significant ordinal association.

Conclusion

So what do we conclude? In this case we have different tests pointing to somewhat different conclusions. The chi-square test, which assumes that the variables are merely nominal-level variables (i.e., the numbers assigned to different values are arbitrary and meaningless), suggests that the data are consistent with the null hypothesis: That is, there is no strong evidence of any relationship or association between ideology and optimism/pessimism. On the other hand, the values of Somers' d and gamma, and the hypothesis tests associated with them, suggest that there *is* a significant relationship between the variables—if we treat the variables as being *ordinal* in nature—but this relationship is not very strong. It would appear that the evidence in favor of the congressional candidate's statement is very weak at best.

It is worth pausing here for a moment to consider a larger lesson suggested by this example. You might think that for any given data set and any given research question, there is *one right way* to analyze the data. This is more or less true, for practical purposes, in many situations, but there are plenty of other cases in which knowledgeable researchers and statisticians can and do reasonably disagree. One common issue underlying such disagreements concerns assumptions about the nature of the variables in question. In the present example researchers might disagree about whether it is appropriate to treat the 3-level measure of optimism-pessimism as an ordinal variable or merely a nominal one—and thus whether one should focus on the chi-square test results (which assumes nominal variables) or the tests of Somers' d or gamma (which assume ordinal variables). Indeed, some researchers would argue that one or both of these variables might reasonably be regarded as *scale* variables rather than merely ordinal variables, in which case we would use yet another different statistical procedure for examining and testing the relationship between the two variables (specifically, a correlation coefficient, as discussed in a subsequent chapter of this book).

Chapter 7

One-Sample *t*-Test

Sample Problem

An expert from the United States Census Bureau claimed during a talk on campus that in 2008, Americans read online newspapers far less, on average, than did Americans at the turn of the century. According to the 2000 Census, Americans read an online newspaper an average of 2 days per week. It just so happens that the ANES includes a question asking respondents to report the number of days in the past week in which they read a daily online newspaper (the variable named *Newspaper*). We are thus able to put the expert's assertion to a test. Is the general population's average number of weekly-read online newspapers in 2008 significantly different from the number of weekly-read online newspapers in 2000?

Statistical Analysis

The null hypothesis in this problem is that the mean of the population for the variable *Newspaper* equals 2; the alternative (research) hypothesis is that it is not equal to 2 (and, more specifically, that is something <2). To evaluate these hypotheses, we obviously will want to look at the mean of *Newspaper* in the ANES 2008 sample; if it is <2, this would be consistent with the research hypothesis. To reject the null hypothesis with confidence, however, we need to conduct a statistical hypothesis test to determine whether the difference between our observed sample mean and the null-hypothesis mean (2) is larger than can reasonably be accounted for by random sampling variation. That is, even if the population mean were 2, the mean of a random sample taken from the population (like ours) would probably not be exactly equal to 2, but rather would be a little smaller or larger than 2 by some random amount.

The appropriate test here is a *one-sample t-test*, which computes how far our sample mean is from the hypothesized value of 2 and compares this to an estimate (based on the data) of random error in the sample estimate. If the computed value of t is larger than would be expected due simply to chance— i.e., if the probability of obtaining a t value this large by chance is very small (e.g., <.05 or .01)—we can reject the null hypothesis with confidence.

Running the Analysis in SPSS

Open SPSS and retrieve the ANES 2008 data file described in Chapter 3 (or, alternatively, one of the revised versions of it that you created in previous chapters). Then, be sure to set SPSS *options* per our instructions in Chapter 2.

Click on **Analyze** on the menu bar, and then choose **Compare Means**. From the resulting menu, choose **One-Sample *t*-Test . . . .** This produces a dialog box that looks like Figure 7.1. In the left-hand box, click on **Newspaper,** then click on the right-arrow button between the boxes to move **Newspaper** to the box labeled "Test Variable(s)." Next, click in the box labeled "Test Value" and edit its contents (which appear as **0** initially) so it reads **2**. This is the null hypothesis value against which you are testing the sample mean. (Of course, you would just leave this box as **0** if you wanted to test the hypothesis that the mean number of days of online newspaper reading equals 0, but that is not what we want to do here.) Now click on **OK** and the analysis will run.

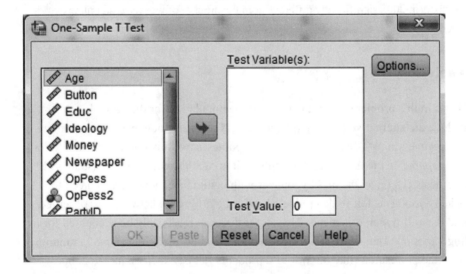

Figure 7.1 Main dialog box for One-Sample t-Test analysis

Output

The output produced by SPSS for the sample problem is shown in Figure 7.2. SPSS first prints some descriptive statistics for the variable *Newspaper,* including number of cases, mean, standard deviation, and standard error. Beneath the descriptive statistics are the results of the significance test. "Mean Difference" is the difference between the observed sample mean (1.01) and the hypothesized mean (2.00). SPSS also prints out a 95% confidence interval for the difference between means, which in this case goes from −1.11 to −0.87.

T-Test

One-Sample Statistics

	N	Mean	Std. Deviation	Std. Error Mean
Newspaper	1156	1.01	2.050	.060

One-Sample Test

	Test Value = 2					
					95% Confidence Interval of the Difference	
	t	df	Sig. (2-tailed)	Mean Difference	Lower	Upper
Newspaper	-16.442	1155	.000	-.991	-1.11	-.87

Figure 7.2 Output from One-Sample t-Test analysis

Is a mean difference of −0.991 large enough to be significantly different from 2? The results of the *t*-test show that $t = -16.422$, with 1155 ($N - 1$) degrees of freedom ("df"). The two-tailed *p*-value for this result is .000 (rounded off to three decimal places). The result is considered statistically significant if the *p*-value is less than the chosen alpha level (usually .05 or .01). In this case, *p* is definitely <.05 (and .01), so the result is considered statistically significant and the null hypothesis is rejected. It appears as though Americans in 2008 do read newspapers online on average less than Americans did at the turn of the century.

If you were doing the problem by hand, you would use a table in your statistics textbook to determine the critical *t*-value associated with 1155 degrees of freedom—this value is 1.96 (for alpha = .05)—and then compare the observed *t*-value to the critical value. In this case, the observed *t* of −16.422 is greater than the critical value (ignore the negative sign in this case), so again you would have rejected the null hypothesis.

Conclusion

It appears that the expert is correct. If the mean number of online newspapers read per week in 2000 was 2, then such readership clearly dropped substantially (and significantly) between then and the time of the ANES 2008 survey.

Please note that like the rest of this fictional example, we made up the part about the 2000 Census data. We have no idea whether that Census showed a mean of 2.0 for online-newspaper readership, or even whether such a question was asked! The ANES data, however, and the observed sample mean of 1.01, are of course quite real.

Chapter 8

Independent-Samples *t*-Test

Sample Problem

When John McCain picked Sarah Palin as his running mate in 2008, some political commentators argued that having a woman on the ticket could help McCain close the gender gap (which we looked at in Chapter 5). The argument was that women, regardless of their political stripes, would be strongly attracted to another woman, while some men might actually be turned off by having a woman at the top of the ticket. In short, it was argued that women would feel warmer toward Palin than would men because Palin was a woman. The ANES includes the variables *TPalin* and *Sex*, which we will use to test this proposition. Do men and women differ with respect to their feeling thermometer ratings of Sarah Palin?

Statistical Analysis

In this problem, we are testing the null hypothesis that there is no difference in mean feeling thermometer ratings for Sarah Palin between men and women in the population. The alternative (research) hypothesis reflects those political commentators' beliefs that the average feeling thermometer rating for Sarah Palin between men and women are not equal—specifically, that women's mean ratings are higher than men's. To examine these hypotheses, we will of course want to look at the ANES 2008 means for men and women separately on *TPalin* to see if they are equal or not— whether the difference between these means equals zero or not. To reject the null hypothesis with confidence, however, we need to conduct a statistical hypothesis test to determine whether the difference between our observed men's and women's means is larger than can reasonably be accounted for by random sampling variation. That is, even if the difference between these means in the population were zero, the mean difference observed in a random sample taken from the population (like ours) would probably not be exactly equal to zero, but rather would be a little smaller or larger than zero by some random amount. The appropriate test here is an *independent-samples t-test*, which computes how far our sample mean difference is from the hypothesized value of zero, and compares this observed difference to an estimate (based on the data) of random error in the sample estimate. If the computed value of *t* is larger than would be expected due simply to chance—that is if the probability of obtaining a *t* value this large by chance is very small (e.g., <.05 or .01)—we can reject the null hypothesis with confidence and conclude that the population mean difference is not zero or, in other words, that there really is a difference between men's and women's average ratings of Sarah Palin.

Running the Analysis in SPSS

Open SPSS and retrieve the ANES 2008 data file described in Chapter 3 (or, alternatively, one of the revised versions of it that you created in previous chapters). Then, be sure to set SPSS *options* per our instructions in Chapter 2.

Click on **Analyze** on the menu bar, and then choose **Compare Means**. From the resulting menu, choose **Independent-Samples *t*-Test** . . . . This produces a dialog box that looks like Figure 8.1.

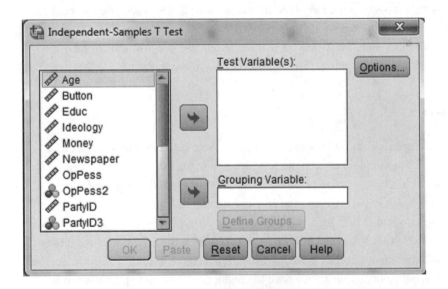

Figure 8.1 Main dialog box for Independent-Samples t-Test analysis

In this dialog box, your list of variables appears in the box to the left, and you must (1) move one (or more) of the variables into the box labeled "Test Variable(s)" to select your dependent variable(s) and (2) move *one* of your variables into the box labeled "Grouping Variable" to identify the groups to be compared (that is, to select the independent variable). First, click on **TPalin** (the dependent variable in our example) in the left-hand box to select it; then click on the upper right-arrow button pointing to the "Test Variable(s)" box; **TPalin** disappears from the left-hand box and reappears under "Test Variable(s)." Next, click on **Sex** (the independent variable in our example) to select it, and then click on the right-arrow button pointing to the "Grouping Variable" box to move it there. The name **Sex** now appears under "Grouping Variable," followed by a set of parentheses containing two question marks. This is to call your attention to the fact that one additional specification is required before you can execute this analysis.

When you selected **Sex** as your grouping variable, something else happened on your screen as well. The button labeled **Define Groups . . .** suddenly looked different. Whereas it previously appeared fuzzy and with lightly colored lettering, it now appears sharp and distinct. This is because the button was not functional until you selected the grouping variable—but it is now functional and quite important. Click on it and another dialog box appears (see Figure 8.2) in which you must specify the two values of **Sex** that represent the two groups you wish to compare. In our case, **Sex** was coded simply as **1** (Male) and **2** (Female). Click in the box next to "Group 1" and, when the cursor appears there, type the number **1**. Then use the mouse to click in the box next to "Group 2" and type the number **2**. Now click on **Continue** to return to the dialog box illustrated in Figure 8.1. In this box, click on **OK** to run the analysis.

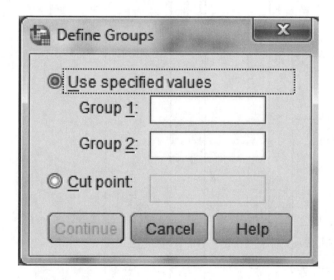

Figure 8.2 Dialog box for defining groups in Independent Samples t-Test analysis

Output

The output produced by SPSS for the sample problem is shown in Figure 8.3.

T-Test

Group Statistics

	Sex	N	Mean	Std. Deviation	Std. Error Mean
TPalin	1 1. Male respondent selected	855	48.53	26.868	.919
	2 2. Female respondent selected	1127	48.17	27.168	.809

Independent Samples Test

		Levene's Test for Equality of Variances		t-test for Equality of Means					95% Confidence Interval of the Difference	
		F	Sig.	t	df	Sig. (2-tailed)	Mean Difference	Std. Error Difference	Lower	Upper
TPalin	Equal variances assumed	.218	.641	.294	1980	.769	.360	1.226	-2.045	2.765
	Equal variances not assumed			.294	1848.966	.769	.360	1.224	-2.041	2.761

Figure 8.3 Output from Independent Samples t-Test analysis

SPSS first prints the number of cases, means, standard deviations, and standard errors on the dependent variable separately for each group. In this case, the two groups are defined by the variable *sex* (1 = male; 2 = female). The results show that the mean for men is higher (48.53) than the mean for women (48.17), although the differences are very, very small.

"Levene's Test for Equality of Variances" is provided next by SPSS. This test is probably not of interest to most readers. (It represents a test of the hypothesis that the populations from which the groups were sampled have equal variances.)

Beneath (or to the right of) Levene's Test are the results of the "*t*-test for Equality of Means." The information provided in the row labeled "Equal variances not assumed" reports the results of a *t*-test that is sometimes used when there is reason to believe that the two population variances are not equal. SPSS reports the observed *t*-value, the degrees of freedom ("df"), and the two-tailed *p*-value ("Sig. [2-tailed]"). This test is not often discussed in introductory statistics courses, so if you have not discussed the test in class, just ignore this part of the output. Also reported on this line are the difference between the means, standard error of the difference, and the 95% confidence interval for the difference between population means.

The most commonly used test is the one listed in the row labeled "Equal variances assumed." Because we are assuming that the two population variances are equal, a pooled variance estimate is used to combine the two sample variances to obtain the most accurate estimate of the variance common to both populations.

The observed *t*-value for this problem is 0.294, with degrees of freedom (total sample size minus 2) equal to 1980. The two-tailed probability of .769 is greater (by a large amount) than .05 and, therefore, the test is not considered significant. In other words, the assumption made by the political commentators that women would give Sarah Palin a higher feeling thermometer rating than men appears not to be the case.

To verify this, you can use your statistics textbook to determine the critical *t*-value associated with 1980 degrees of freedom: The critical value of *t*, using alpha = .05, equals approximately 1.96. The observed *t*-value (0.294) is lower than the critical *t*-value; therefore we fail to reject the null hypothesis.

Conclusion

Contrary to what many people seem to have assumed, there is no evidence that women like Sarah Palin any more than men do—at least at the time of the ANES 2008 survey. The observed difference between men's and women's mean feeling thermometer ratings of Palin was very small, and clearly not any larger than could be explained by random sampling error.

Chapter 9

Correlations

Sample Problem

Walking back to their dorm rooms after listening to a lecture on why people engage in political activities beyond simply voting, two students debate the relative relationship between education and age. One student believes that age is related to political activities beyond voting, while the other believes that education is related to political activities beyond voting. They decided to make a detour to the social sciences research lab to see which one was right.

In addition to containing measures of *Age* and *Educ*, which we will need for our analysis, the ANES includes several variables that measure participation in various political activities, including talking to other people about voting (the variable named *Talk* in the version of the data set we have provided for you); attending rallies, speeches, and so forth (*Rally*); wearing campaign buttons or posting signs (*Button*); working for a party or candidate (*Work*); and contributing money to a campaign (*Money*). Because our question is about "political activities" generally, it will be useful to combine these five variables together into a scale for use in our analysis. Specifically, we are interested in calculating *correlations* between this new measure of political activity and the variables *Age* and *Educ*, respectively, and determining whether the correlations calculated on the sample are statistically significantly different from zero.

Statistical Analysis

In this chapter we are going to use a *correlation analysis* to examine each student's hypothesis separately. Correlation analysis allows us to measure the degree to which any two variables, both measured at the *scale* level, are statistically related to one another. In our case, we have a scale of political participation (which we will create in the next section), and two scale-level variables already in the ANES data: *Age* and *Educ*. One student predicts that the new variable will be correlated with *Age*; the other expects the new variable to be correlated with *Educ*. Either student might be right—or both, or neither.

The statistic we will use to measure the degree of relationship between scale-level variables is the *Pearson product-moment correlation coefficient* (hereafter referred to as the "correlation coefficient" or simply "correlation"). Correlation coefficients range from −1.0 to +1.0. A value of zero means there is no relationship at all between the variables. A *positive* value for the

74

correlation means that respondents who have relatively high scores on one variable tend, on average, to have relatively high scores on the other (and, conversely, low scores tend to be paired with low scores). For example, a positive correlation between *Age* and *Educ* would mean that, on average, older people tend to have more education than do younger people or, to say it another way, more educated people tend to be older than less educated people. A *negative* correlation means that the relationship is in the opposite direction, such that people with high scores on one variable tend to have low scores on the other, and vice-versa. The *strength* of the relationship is represented by the magnitude of the correlation. A correlation near zero means a very weak relationship, whereas larger values (in either direction) reflect stronger relationships.

As with most other statistical procedures, the statistic (in this case, correlation coefficient) computed on a sample (ANES) is only an *estimate* of the true value in the population from which the sample was obtained. What we really want to know is what the correlation is in the population. In particular, we are usually interested in the key question of whether the correlation in the population is zero or not. Are the two variables related to each other or not? The correlation analysis in SPSS will provide us with not only the (sample) correlation coefficients of interest, but also a significance test for reach. The null hypothesis for such a test is that the population correlation is zero (i.e., the variables are unrelated to each other). The two students in our example are each hoping to be able to reject this null hypothesis for the particular pair of variables about which they made their respective predictions, and thus be able to conclude that a relationship does exist between the variables as predicted.

Running the Analysis in SPSS

Open SPSS and retrieve the ANES 2008 data file described in Chapter 3 (or, alternatively, one of the revised versions of it that you created in previous chapters). Then, be sure to set SPSS *options* per our instructions in Chapter 2.

Data Transformations

Before computing our new political-activity variable, we will need to recode each of them so that when we add them together into a scale, they will produce a measure of political activities that we can make some sense out of. To see why this is important, follow the procedures described in Chapter 4 to create a frequency distribution for each of the variables *Talk*, *Rally*, *Button*, *Work*, and *Money*. The frequency table for the first of these, *Talk*, is shown in Figure 9.1. There are two things to notice here. First, the *Talk* variable is dichotomous—responses are simply "yes" or "no."

Frequencies

Talk

		Frequency	Percent	Valid Percent	Cumulative Percent
Valid	1 1. Yes	904	38.9	43.0	43.0
	5 5. No	1197	51.5	57.0	100.0
	Total	2101	90.4	100.0	
Missing	-8 -8. Don't know	1	.0		
	-2 -2. No Post-election IW	221	9.5		
	Total	222	9.6		
Total		2323	100.0		

Figure 9.1 Output from Frequencies analysis for 'Talk' variable

Second, the answer "yes" is coded as the number *1*, and the answer "no" is coded as the number *5*. The same is true for the other four variables (not shown). If we were to just add up scores on the five variables, we would have a very odd scale in which someone who participated in all five types of activities would have a total participation score of 5 (which makes sense), but someone who did not participate in any of them would have a total participation score of 25 (which does not make much sense). What we will want to do is change all of these 5s ("no" responses) to 0s, so that now "yes" is coded 1 and "no" is coded 0. Now, when we add the five activities together into a scale, we will create a new variable ranging from 0 (respondent did none of the activities) to 5 (respondent did all five activities), with intermediate values representing intermediate levels of participation.

To do this, follow the *Recode* procedure outlined in Chapter 2 (and used in Chapters 4 and 5 for other variables) to recode each of the five variables "into different variables." To make things easy to follow, recode *Talk* into *Talk2*, *Rally* into *Rally2*, and so on. For each, recode the value of 1 into 1 (i.e., no change to the "yes" responses) and recode the value 5 into 0.

Once you complete your recoding procedure, it might be a good idea to make sure the recoding was done properly by producing frequency distributions for your new variables and comparing them to the distributions of the original variables: The only thing that should be different between the two is that "no" in the original variables will be coded as 5, but in the new variables it will be coded as 0.

Now, use the *Compute* procedure outlined in Chapter 2 to combine the five new variables you just recoded into a new index variable of political activities, and name the new variable *PartIndex*. Specifically, we want to compute *PartIndex* as the sum of *Talk2*, *Rally2*, *Button2*, *Work2*, and *Money2*—that is, **Talk2 + Rally2 + Button2 + Work2 + Money2**.

Once you have completed this procedure, create a frequency distribution for this new variable. The frequency distribution should look like Figure 9.2. Note that scores on the variable range from 0 (engaged in none of the activities) to 5 (engaged in all of the activities). Nearly half of the respondents (998, or a valid percentage of 47.5%) have scores of zero, 668 respondents (valid percent = 31.8%), and so on.

Frequencies

PartIndex

		Frequency	Percent	Valid Percent	Cumulative Percent
Valid	.00	998	43.0	47.5	47.5
	1.00	668	28.8	31.8	79.4
	2.00	259	11.1	12.3	91.7
	3.00	91	3.9	4.3	96.0
	4.00	49	2.1	2.3	98.4
	5.00	34	1.5	1.6	100.0
	Total	2099	90.4	100.0	
Missing	System	224	9.6		
Total		2323	100.0		

Figure 9.2 Output from Frequencies analysis for new 'PartIndex' variable

Now that we have created our participation-index variable, we are ready to turn to the desired analysis, namely computing correlations between our new *PartIndex* variable and the ANES variables *Age* and *Educ*.

Running the Analysis

Click on **Analyze** on the menu bar, and then choose **Correlate**. From the resulting menu, choose **Bivariate . . . .** This produces a dialog box that looks like Figure 9.3.

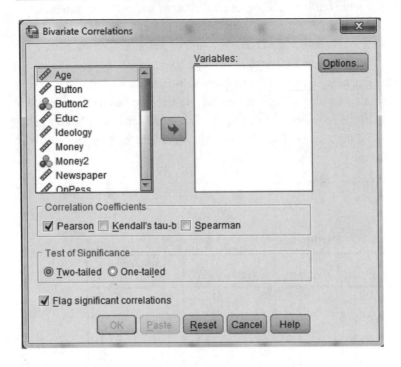

Figure 9.3 Main dialog box for Correlations analysis

The rest is fairly self-explanatory. As in previous procedures, choose the variables you wish to include in the analyses by moving them from the box on the left to the box on the right (under "Variables"). Click on a variable name (say, **Age**), and then click on the right-arrow key in the center of the dialog box. Repeat this for the next two variables **Educ** and **PartIndex**. For the present example, we selected the variables in the order in which we entered them into the data window, but this is not necessary. The order of selection influences only the order in which the variables are listed in the output.

As you can see from the checked boxes in Figure 9.3, clicking **OK** to run the analysis without changing anything else produces (1) Pearson correlation coefficients rather than Kendall's tau-b or Spearman coefficients, (2) two-tailed rather than one-tailed significance tests, and (3) a display in which SPSS will "flag significant correlations." ("Flag significant correlations" asks SPSS to print an asterisk next to each correlation that is significant at the .05 level, so you can locate these significant correlations easily when examining the output.) Click in the appropriate boxes to change any of these settings if you wish; clicking on a box that is already selected (already has a check mark in it) will unselect it. For this example we will leave all of these options at their default values.

If you wish to also see means and standard deviations for the variables selected, click on **Options . . .** , then click on the box labeled "Means and Standard Deviations" in the resulting dialog window (not shown). Click on **Continue** to exit this window, then on **OK** to run the analysis.

Output

The output produced by SPSS for the Pearson correlations analysis is shown in Figure 9.4.

Correlations

Correlations

		Age	Educ	PartIndex
Age	Pearson Correlation	1	-.133**	.045*
	Sig. (2-tailed)		.000	.040
	N	2301	2291	2080
Educ	Pearson Correlation	-.133**	1	.226**
	Sig. (2-tailed)	.000		.000
	N	2291	2312	2090
PartIndex	Pearson Correlation	.045*	.226**	1
	Sig. (2-tailed)	.040	.000	
	N	2080	2090	2099

**. Correlation is significant at the 0.01 level (2-tailed).
*. Correlation is significant at the 0.05 level (2-tailed).

Figure 9.4 Output from Correlations analysis

SPSS produces a correlation matrix showing the correlations between all possible pairs of variables and indicates the number of cases used to compute them. In each cell of the correlation matrix—that is, at each intersection of a given row and column—appear three pieces of information. The top number is the correlation coefficient itself; the number below this is the two-tailed p-value for the correlation; and the bottom number is the sample size (N) on which the correlation is based. Looking at the extreme upper-right corner, for example, we see that the correlation between *Age* and *PartIndex* equals .045, that $p = .040$, and that this is based on 2,080 cases (respondents). A correlation coefficient of .045 is quite small, indicating a rather weak relationship between the variables; however, it is significantly different from zero according to a two-tailed test at the .05 alpha level. (The reason for this is that the sample size is so large, which means that a correlation does not have to be very different from zero to be significant.) The next cell down shows that the correlation between *Educ* and *PartIndex* equals .226, that $p = .000$ (i.e., <.0005), and that this is based on 2,090 cases. Thus, this correlation, which would be considered moderately strong, is significantly different from zero according to a two-tailed test at both the .05 and .01 alpha levels.

You will have noticed the redundancy in the table—each correlation appears twice in the square matrix, as the upper-right triangle is a mirror image of the lower-left triangle. The correlation between X and Y is the same as the correlation between Y and X. The correlation coefficient does not distinguish between these cases. The same information about the *Age–PartIndex* correlation is printed in the extreme lower-left corner as well. (This seems like a lot of wasted ink to us, but it was not up to us.)

Conclusion

So what do we conclude? It would appear that *both* education and age are related to political activity beyond voting. It should also be noted, however, that education appears to be more strongly related to political activity beyond voting (with a significant correlation of .226) than is age (with a significant but much smaller correlation of .045). So both students were correct, but one certainly has more bragging rights than the other!

Chapter 10

Simple Linear Regression

Sample Problem

In Chapter 9, our fictional students found that the level of education is correlated with the level of engagement in political activities, specifically, that there was a moderately strong positive correlation (.226) between the ANES variable *Educ* and the new variable (*PartIndex*) that we created from other ANES variables. On average, people with more education get involved in political activities more than people with less education. If the two variables are statistically related in this way, then it stands to reason that knowing a person's level of education would, to some extent, be useful information for predicting his or her level of political participation. (The reverse would be equally true, but it makes more sense to us to think of education level influencing political activity than the other way around.) The students therefore decide to further explore this link between education and political activity using *simple linear regression.*

The word "regression" in this phrase refers to a particular statistical procedure for predicting values on a variable from values on one or more other variables; the word "linear" means that we will do so using an equation representing a straight line (i.e., to ask how much change in one variable is associated, on average, with a given amount of change in the other variable) and the word "simple," means that we are predicting a variable from just one predictor variable. In Chapter 11, we will discuss *multiple* linear regression, which involves predicting one variable from two or more predictors. In Chapter 12, we will discuss *logistic* regression which, in contrast to *linear* regression, uses a nonlinear equation to predict a variable from one or more predictors.

Statistical Analysis

As discussed in the previous chapter, correlation coefficients tell us the magnitude and direction of a relationship on an intuitive and familiar scale from −1.0 to 0 to +1.0. Recall also that the correlation coefficient is a *nondirectional statistic*. The correlation between X and Y means exactly the same thing as the correlation between Y and X. For many purposes, this is all we need to know about the relationship between two scale-level variables, but for other purposes it is useful to view the problem from a different perspective and ask how, and how well, one can predict one of the variables (the *dependent* or *criterion* variable) from the other (the *independent* or *predictor* variable). To do this, we use *simple linear regression*, which, as we will see, is (not surprisingly) very closely related to correlation.

The idea behind simple linear regression is to find a linear mathematical equation that does the best job of predicting scores on the dependent variable (in this case, *PartIndex*) from scores on the independent variable (*Educ*). You probably recall from high school algebra that the form of a linear equation (for a straight line, in graphical terms) is "$Y = mX + b$," where m represents the slope of the line and b represents the Y-intercept—the value of Y when $X = 0$. (We hope you are not too attached to the idea that the slope is "m" and the intercept is "b"; in the field of Statistics, generally, and in SPSS specifically, it is conventional to use different letters, as we will explain later in this chapter.) In regression analysis, we will find a line (equation) that does the best job, mathematically speaking, of describing the relationship between the variables. Of particular interest to us will be the *slope* of this line, which tells us how much (on average) Y changes when X changes by one unit. In this case, how much the *PartIndex* variable increases, on average, with each additional year of education. Once we have such an equation, we can easily substitute any value for education (the X variable in this case) into the equation to compute a predicted *PartIndex* score. In addition, we will be able to (1) assess how *good* our prediction actually is using this equation, and (2) test the null hypothesis that, in the population from which the sample was drawn, th.e slope of the prediction line is 0 (X scores and Y scores are unrelated or, to say it in another way, X scores are of no use in predicting Y scores).

Running the Analysis in SPSS

Open SPSS and retrieve the (modified) data file that you created in Chapter 9 for the correlation problem which includes the new *PartIndex* variable that we need again in this chapter. If you did not save that file, you will have to first go through the steps outlined in Chapter 9 to create *PartIndex* using *Recode* and *Compute* commands. Then, be sure to set SPSS *options* per our instructions in Chapter 2.

Now, click on **Analyze** on the menu bar, and then choose **Regression**. From the resulting menu, choose **Linear . . . .** This produces a dialog box that looks like Figure 10.1.

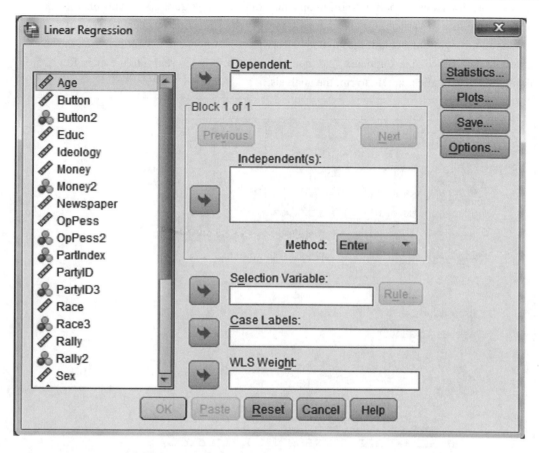

Figure 10.1 Main dialog box for Linear Regression analysis

The rest of the procedure is straightforward. As in previous procedures, choose the variables you wish to include in the analyses by moving them, one by one, from the box in which they appear on the left to either the "Dependent" box or the "Independent(s)" box on the right. In the present example, *PartIndex* is the dependent variable, so click on **PartIndex** in the left box and then on the right-arrow button pointing to the "Dependent" box. Our independent variable is **Educ**, so click on it (in the left box) and then click on the right-arrow button pointing to the "Independent(s)" box.

At this point, you may click on **OK** to run the analysis, or proceed one additional step to ask SPSS to print the means and standard deviations for the variables selected, as well as the Pearson correlation between them, along with your regression analysis results. To obtain these statistics, click on the **Statistics . . .** button to bring up a new dialog box (Figure 10.2). This dialog box contains two lists of various sorts of options, some of which are already checked. One of these options in the right-hand column is labeled "Descriptives." Choose this by clicking on the box to its left so that a check mark appears, and then click on **Continue** to return to the main Regression dialog box. Then, click on **OK** to run the analysis.

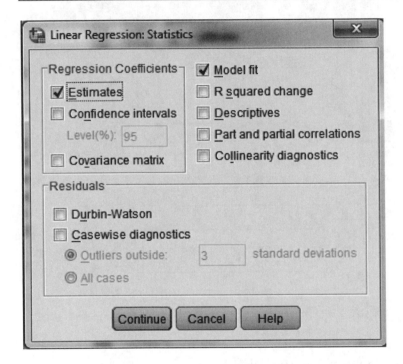

Figure 10.2 Dialog box for specifying statistics in Linear Regression analysis

Scatterplots

It is always a good idea to visually examine the scatterplot of the two variables when interpreting a regression analysis. To obtain a scatterplot with *PartIndex* on the *Y*- (vertical) axis and *Educ* on the *X*- (horizontal) axis, click on **Graphs** on the menu bar at the top of the screen, then on **Legacy Dialogs,** and then click **Scatter/Dot . . .** on the resulting pull down menu. This produces a small dialog box picturing five kinds of scatterplots, as illustrated in Figure 10.3. The plot type we want, "Simple scatter," is already selected by default. Click on the **Define** button to produce another dialog box (see Figure 10.4) in which your variables are listed in the box to the left. Click on **PartIndex**, and then click on the right-arrow button pointing to "*Y*

Axis." Then, click on **Educ** and click on the right-arrow button pointing to "*X* Axis." Then, click on **OK** to generate the scatterplot.

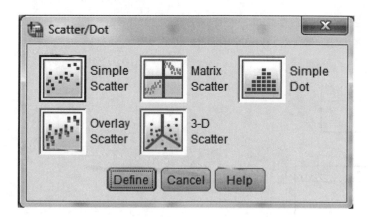

Figure 10.3 Main dialog box for Graphs

Figure 10.4 Dialog box for specifying Scatterplots

Output

The output produced by SPSS for the sample problem, including the optional descriptive statistics, is shown in Figure 10.5.

Regression

Descriptive Statistics

	Mean	Std. Deviation	N
PartIndex	.8699	1.10800	2090
Educ	13.13	2.569	2090

Correlations

		PartIndex	Educ
Pearson Correlation	PartIndex	1.000	.226
	Educ	.226	1.000
Sig. (1-tailed)	PartIndex	.	.000
	Educ	.000	.
N	PartIndex	2090	2090
	Educ	2090	2090

Model Summary

Model	R	R Square	Adjusted R Square	Std. Error of the Estimate
1	.226[a]	.051	.051	1.07952

a. Predictors: (Constant), Educ

ANOVA[b]

Model		Sum of Squares	df	Mean Square	F	Sig.
1	Regression	131.313	1	131.313	112.680	.000[a]
	Residual	2433.288	2088	1.165		
	Total	2564.601	2089			

a. Predictors: (Constant), Educ
b. Dependent Variable: PartIndex

Coefficients[a]

Model		Unstandardized Coefficients		Standardized Coefficients	t	Sig.
		B	Std. Error	Beta		
1	(Constant)	-.412	.123		-3.346	.001
	Educ	.098	.009	.226	10.615	.000

a. Dependent Variable: PartIndex

Figure 10.5 Output from Linear Regression analysis

If you requested descriptive statistics, these are printed first. The means, standard deviations, number of cases, and a correlation matrix are produced for the two variables *PartIndex* and *Educ*. The correlation between these two variables is .226 (exactly as we found in Chapter 9), which indicates a moderately strong, positive relationship, such that people with higher levels of education engage in more political activities on average than people with lower levels of education.

Following a small section titled "Variables Entered/Removed" (not shown here), SPSS produces regression analysis statistics, including the multiple correlation coefficient ("R"), R^2 ("R Square"), *adjusted* or *shrunken* R^2 ("Adjusted R Square"), and the *standard error of the estimate*. Note that in simple regression, in which only one predictor variable is used, the multiple R is equivalent to the simple correlation between the two variables—in this case, .226. Squaring this value produces *Multiple* R^2, representing the proportion of variance in the dependent variable predictable from the independent variable. We will see in the next chapter that these statistics are much more informative, or at least less redundant with what we already knew from the correlation coefficient, when we include more than one predictor variable in the equation.

An analysis of variance (ANOVA) table for the regression equation is produced next; this represents a test of the null hypothesis that *Multiple R* (or, equivalently, R^2) in the population equals 0. The variance of the dependent variable is partitioned into two sources: the part predictable from the regression equation ("Regression") and the part not predictable from the equation ("Residual" or error). The *F*-test is significant ($F = 112.680$, with 1 and 2088 degrees of freedom and a *p*-value ("Sig.") of .000. There are two interesting things to note here. First, if you divide the sum of squares due to regression (131.313) by the "total" sum of squares total, the sum of squares for regression and the sum of squares residual (2564.601) equal the value of R^2 (.051). This is why R^2 literally represents the proportion of variance in the dependent variable that is predictable from the independent variable. Second, given that the *Multiple R* is equivalent to the simple correlation between X and Y, it should come as no surprise that the significance tests are the same as well. Although it is difficult to tell precisely from this example, the "Sig." value for this F test of .000 (rounded off) is equivalent to that for the correlation coefficient (as per the previous chapter). Again, this will change in the next chapter, when we include additional predictor variables in multiple linear regression.

The final section of the output provides the information needed to construct the regression (prediction) equation for predicting *PartIndex* scores from *Educ* scores. The column labeled "B" lists the regression coefficients for the independent variable *Educ* and for the "Constant" term. These represent the slope and *Y*-intercept, respectively, for the regression line. As we noted near the beginning of this chapter, the old "$Y = mX = b$" formula undergoes something of a makeover in statistics: The coefficients "m" and "b" are usually both represented by the letter "b," with different subscripts, and the terms are (by convention) reordered, so that the linear regression equation is written instead as follows:

$$\text{Predicted value on } Y = b_0 + b_1 * X,$$

In this representation, the Y-intercept, which SPSS labels as "constant," is represented by b_0, and the slope is represented by b_1. Substituting the names of our variables, and the respective "B" coefficients from the SPSS output, yields the following regression equation:

$$\text{Predicted } PartIndex = (-.412) + (.098) * Educ$$

Note that we have added parentheses only for visual clarity. The slope (b_1) coefficient for *Educ* means that, on average, an increase of one unit (year) of education is associated with (predicts) an increase of .098 political activities (on a 1–5 scale) on the *PartIndex* variable.

The values listed under "Beta" represent an alternative set of coefficients that would be used instead, if all variables were first converted to Z-scores—if they were first standardized to have a mean of 0 and a standard deviation of 1. Note that here there is no value for "Constant" in this column: If both variables are in Z-score form, the Y-intercept is always 0. Thus, the prediction equation for predicting Z-scores on Y from Z-scores on X is

$$\text{Predicted } Z_{PARTINDEX} = 0 + (.226) * Z_{EDUC}$$

or more simply:

$$\text{Predicted } Z_{PARTINDEX} = (.226) * Z_{EDUC}$$

This means, literally, that as *Educ* increases by one standard deviation, *PartIndex* increases on average by about one-fourth of a standard deviation (precisely, .226 standard deviations). Also note that the value of .226 might sound familiar: It is exactly the same as the correlation coefficient between the two variables! This will always be the case in *simple* linear regression, when there is only one predictor variable, but again, this will change when we introduce multiple regression in the next chapter. In that case, the beta coefficients are not equivalent to any particular correlation coefficients, but rather provide important and unique information about how the various predictor variables relate to (predict) the dependent variable.

Finally, the last two columns of this table report the results of the significance tests for each coefficient. The null hypothesis being tested on each line is that the particular b coefficient (or the beta coefficient—the tests are equivalent) equals 0 in the population. The t- and p-values for these tests are labeled "t" and "Sig.," respectively. The p-values are reported as ".001" and ".000," respectively. Both coefficients (the slope b_1 and the intercept b_0) are significantly different from 0 (although we are usually not interested in the test for the intercept term). Because there is only one predictor variable, the significance test for the slope (for the variable *Educ*) turns out to be identical to the significance test for the correlation coefficient which, as noted earlier, is also equivalent to the significance test for *Multiple R*. Again, we have in some ways simply rediscovered correlation, but (also again) this will change in multiple regression.

Scatterplots

Figure 10.6 shows a scatterplot of variables *PartIndex* and *Educ*. Each point represents a research subject: The vertical location of the point represents the subject's score on *PartIndex*, and the horizontal location represents his or her score on *Educ*. With a little imagination, perhaps you can "see" how a straight line that best fits the data would have a slightly positive slope from left to right.

Graph

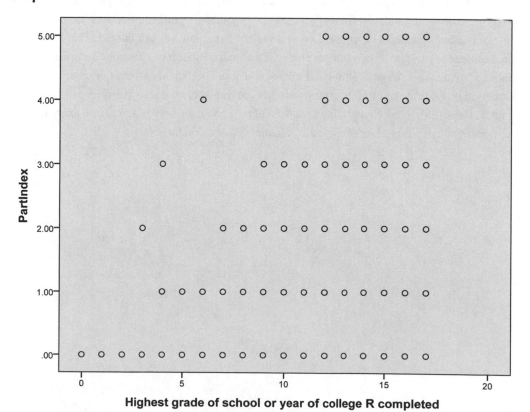

Figure 10.6 Output from Scatterplot analysis

Conclusion

So, what do we conclude? We can reject the null hypothesis that, in the population from which the sample was drawn, the slope of the prediction line between education and political activity is 0, and instead conclude with a high degree of statistical certainty that the predictive relationship between education and political activity is nonzero. According to our sample data, the relationship is moderately strong and positive, such that increased education (on average) predicts increased levels of political activity.

Given the number of ways in which the results of our simple regression have simply replicated what we already knew from the correlation coefficient (and its significance test), you might reasonably wonder why anyone would bother with regression. To be honest, the answer is that it is in fact rare for researchers to conduct *simple* linear regression analyses on their data: If they just want to know about the (linear) relationship between two scale variables, they ordinarily just compute the correlation coefficient (and its corresponding significance test). The main reason for including this chapter in the present book is mainly to prepare you for the next chapter on *multiple* linear regression. When our prediction equation includes more than one independent variable, statistics like *Multiple R*, *b* coefficients, and *beta* coefficients provide unique information that could not be inferred from simply looking at correlations between pairs of variables. Having slogged through this chapter will prove to have been a good investment of your time, when you get ready to handle the next chapter. Trust us on this one.

Chapter 11

Multiple Linear Regression

Sample Problem

In their political science research methods class, the students discussed in the two previous
chapters describe the findings from their correlation and simple regression analyses
(relating political activity to education level), to their professor. Praising their work, the
professor challenges them to go further. What other factors might also predict political activity,
along with education? The professor suggests that they conduct a *multiple regression analysis* to
predict the dependent variable (participation in political activities) from several independent
variables at the same time. Remembering the correlation analysis they conducted earlier
between education, age, and political activity, the two students decide to include age, in addition
to education, as predictors in their new analysis. Moreover, given that they are using data from
2008, they wonder if how people feel about the two presidential candidates (Barack Obama and
John McCain) is also predictive of their level of political activity as well. They are thus going to
use multiple linear regression to predict the dependent variable *PartIndex* from four independent
variables: *Educ*, *Age*, *TObama*, and *TMcCain*.

Statistical Analysis

Multiple linear regression can be thought of as an extension of simple linear regression
(Chapter 10), in which a dependent variable is predicted from two or more
independent/predictor variables (thus "multiple" rather than "simple"). Although simple linear
regression was in many ways no different than correlation, focusing on the relationship between
two variables, multiple regression is extremely important for its ability to provide a plethora of
unique information about the prediction of a dependent variable from numerous
independent/predictor variables. For example, multiple regression allows us to determine how
well the dependent variable can be predicted statistically from a group of variables
collectively—which is quite different from asking how well any particular independent variable
predicts the dependent variable. This is reflected in the multiple R (and R^2) statistic, which is no
longer equivalent to the correlation between any one predictor and the dependent variable. In
addition, and of particular importance, is the fact that the analysis allows us to determine the
degree to which each independent variable contributes to prediction *while holding all of the*

other independent variables constant—the degree to which it predicts independently and uniquely above and beyond the prediction afforded by the other predictor variables in the equation. This is particularly useful when the predictor variables are themselves correlated with one another, or in methodological terms, *confounded* with one another. Multiple regression analysis provides the opportunity to tease apart the unique predictive power of each variable, as if it were not confounded (correlated) with other predictors.

Toward this end, multiple regression analysis tries to find the best equation for predicting the dependent variable from the various independent variables, by assigning different weights (coefficients, or slopes) to each predictor to create the best combination. In general terms, the multiple regression equation looks like this:

$$\text{Predicted } Y = b_0 + b_1 * X_1 + b_2 * X_2 + b_3 * X_3 + \dots$$

Now you can see why, in simple regression, the coefficients were all labeled as "b," but with different subscripts. The first coefficient, b_0, is the Y-intercept or "constant," and then each of the other b values represents the slope ("regression coefficient") for each successive predictor variable. In our present example, we will compute the coefficients for this equation:

$$\text{Predicted } PartIndex = b_0 + b_1 * (Educ) + b_2 * (Age) + b_3 * (TObama) + b_4 * (TMcCain)$$

Another important use of multiple regression involves comparing two hierarchical models— that is, the predictor variables in one model represent a subset of the predictor variables in the other model—against each other. In the present example, for instance, you might want to test the "full" model containing all four predictors with a "reduced" model containing only, say, *Educ*; this comparison would test the hypothesis that *Educ, TObama, and TMcCain collectively* predict additional variance in the dependent variable above and beyond what can be predicted by *Educ* alone. In a final section, we discuss how to conduct such model-comparison tests.

Another popular, but highly controversial, variation on multiple regression analysis involves what are known as "stepwise" selection methods. In these procedures, the user provides a list of potential independent variables and allows SPSS to choose among them based on statistical criteria. Such procedures result in a series of regression analyses in which independent variables are systematically added or subtracted from the equation, one by one, with a new regression equation computed at each step until some predetermined statistical criterion is reached. We are on the side of the controversy that believes these procedures are *not* to be recommended for most purposes; however, we explain how to conduct such analyses if you (or, perhaps more importantly, your instructor) disagree with us.

Running the Analysis in SPSS

Open SPSS and retrieve the (modified) data file that you created in Chapter 9 for the correlation problem, which includes the new *PartIndex* variable that we need again in this chapter. If you did not save that file, you will have to first go through the steps outlined in Chapter 9 to create *PartIndex* using *Recode* and *Compute* commands. Then, be sure to set SPSS *options* per our instructions in Chapter 2.

The procedure for specifying the analysis in SPSS is very similar to that outlined in the Chapter 10 on simple regression. Click on **Analyze** on the menu bar, and then choose **Regression**. From the resulting menu, choose Linear . . . . In the resulting dialog box (illustrated in Figure 10.1 in the previous chapter), move the variable **PartIndex** into the "Dependent" box, and move the variables **Educ**, **Age**, **TObama**, and **TMcCain** into the "Independent(s)" box. To get descriptive statistics (including correlations), click on the **Statistics. . .** button and select "Descriptives" in the resulting dialog box. Click on **Continue** to close this dialog box, then on **OK** to run the analysis.

Hierarchical Model Comparisons

Specification of a comparison between two hierarchical models, as in the example described near the beginning of this chapter, requires two steps, which can be done in either of two ways. One way is to begin by specifying the "full" (larger) model, exactly as described above, including all four predictor variables as "Independent(s)," and then to remove one or more predictors in a second step. For the present example, choose the dependent variable **PartIndex** and all four independent (predictor) variables, as we did above. Before clicking on **OK**, however, click on the button labeled **Next**, which is between the "Dependent" and "Independent(s)" boxes (again, see Figure 10.1). The text to the left of this button will change to say "Block 2 of 2," to indicate that you are now going to specify the second step, and the list of "Independent(s)" will be empty again. Now move the variables **Age**, **TObama**, and **TMcCain** (but not **Educ**) from the left box into the "Independent(s)" box. Click on the downward-pointing arrow text to "Method: Enter," and choose **Remove** from the pull-down menu. Finally, click on the **Statistics . . .** button (at the right in the dialog box), and in the resulting screen, choose the option labeled "R squared change." This important last step asks SPSS to print the results of the crucial test assessing whether the "full," four-predictor model predicts significantly more variance in the dependent variable than does the "reduced" model (from which three predictors were removed). Click on **Continue** to close this dialog box, and then click on **OK** to run the analysis.

The alternative way of conducting this test is essentially the reverse of the first: Instead of beginning with a "full" model and then removing three predictors from it, you begin with the "reduced" model and then ask SPSS to *add* the other predictors at the second step. To do it this way, (1) first specify a one-predictor model, with **Educ** as the only "Independent(s)"; (2) then click on **Next** (to specify the next model); (3) move **Age**, **TObama**, and **TMcCain** to the "Independent(s)" list; (4) change "Method" to **Enter** (rather than **Remove**, as in the preceding paragraph); (5) click on **Statistics . . .** and choose "R squared change"; and finally (6) click **Continue**, then **OK**.

    Whichever of these ways you choose, each section in the resulting output will have separate lines corresponding to "Model 1" and "Model 2"; a section at the beginning of the output will remind you what variables were entered or removed at each step. The section of the output containing the crucial significance test comparing the models is reproduced later in this chapter (see Figure 11.1). The results will be the same either way: If you did it the first way, SPSS will tell us whether removing *Age*, *TObama*, and *TMcCain* (from an equation containing these three variables plus *Educ*) reduces our predictive power; if you did it the second way, the question is simply recast in terms of whether adding those three variables to an equation containing only *Educ* increases our predictive power. They are really just two different ways of asking the exact same question.

Stepwise Variable Selection

To run one of the so-called stepwise procedures, complete the preceding steps for all of the potential independent variables of interest in the "Independent(s)" box. Near the middle of the dialog box you will see the word "Method," and to the right of this, the word "Enter" appears in a small box. To the right of this, in turn, is a small downward-pointing arrow button. Click on this button to produce a pull-down menu that lists several options. (In the analyses above, we chose either **Enter** or **Remove**.) Simply click on **Stepwise, Backward,** or **Forward** to choose one of these stepwise methods; then click on **OK** to run the analysis. (These methods are typically not used often, so they are not taught in this textbook.)

Output

The output produced by SPSS for the sample problem, including the optional descriptive statistics, is shown in Figure 11.1.

Regression

Descriptive Statistics

	Mean	Std. Deviation	N
PartIndex	.8774	1.10986	2047
Educ	13.17	2.519	2047
Age	46.71	16.926	2047
TObama	72.06	26.915	2047
TMcCain	50.75	24.149	2047

Correlations

		PartIndex	Educ	Age	TObama	TMcCain
Pearson Correlation	PartIndex	1.000	.226	.047	.066	-.069
	Educ	.226	1.000	-.108	-.133	.094
	Age	.047	-.108	1.000	-.029	.106
	TObama	.066	-.133	-.029	1.000	-.420
	TMcCain	-.069	.094	.106	-.420	1.000
Sig. (1-tailed)	PartIndex	.	.000	.016	.001	.001
	Educ	.000	.	.000	.000	.000
	Age	.016	.000	.	.095	.000
	TObama	.001	.000	.095	.	.000
	TMcCain	.001	.000	.000	.000	.
N	PartIndex	2047	2047	2047	2047	2047
	Educ	2047	2047	2047	2047	2047
	Age	2047	2047	2047	2047	2047
	TObama	2047	2047	2047	2047	2047
	TMcCain	2047	2047	2047	2047	2047

Variables Entered/Removed[b]

Model	Variables Entered	Variables Removed	Method
1	TMcCain, Educ, Age, TObama	.	Enter

a. All requested variables entered.
b. Dependent Variable: PartIndex

Regression

Variables Entered/Removed[c]

Model	Variables Entered	Variables Removed	Method
1	TMcCain, Educ, Age, TObama	.	Enter
2	.[a]	TMcCain, TObama, Age	Remove

a. All requested variables entered.
b. All requested variables removed.
c. Dependent Variable: PartIndex

Model Summary

Model	R	R Square	Adjusted R Square	Std. Error of the Estimate	R Square Change	F Change	df1	df2	Sig. F Change
1	.266[a]	.071	.069	1.07096	.071	38.826	4	2042	.000
2	.226[b]	.051	.051	1.08131	-.019	14.231	3	2042	.000

a. Predictors: (Constant), TMcCain, Educ, Age, TObama
b. Predictors: (Constant), Educ

Figure 11.1 Output from Multiple Linear Regression analysis

If you requested descriptive statistics, the means, standard deviations, and number of cases are printed for each variable included in the analysis first, followed by a matrix showing the correlations among all of the variables (along with N's and "Sig." values). Note that the correlation matrix looks similar to that produced by the Correlations procedure discussed in Chapter 9, with one important difference: the "Sig." values are now "one-tailed" probabilities, in contrast to the "two-tailed" probabilities produced (by default) by the *Correlations* procedure. Of greatest interest to us here is the fact that all of the independent variables correlate positively and significantly with the dependent variable (*PartIndex*) except for *TMcCain*, which is actually significantly (though very weakly) correlated with *PartIndex* in a *negative* direction. Considering the variable relationships one at a time, it appears that higher levels of political participation are associated with higher levels of education (correlation of .226, as we have found before), being older (correlation of .047, again as we have seen previously), and higher ratings of Obama (correlation of .066). Greater participation, however, is actually predicted by lower ratings of John McCain (correlation of −.069).

Following a brief section ("Variables Entered/Removed") confirming your analysis specification, SPSS produces regression statistics, including the multiple correlation coefficient ("R"), R^2 ("R Square"), adjusted or shrunken R^2 ("Adjusted R Square"), and the standard error of the estimate. Unlike simple regression, in which only one predictor variable is used, the multiple R is not equivalent to any of the simple pairwise correlations printed previously. Multiple R represents the correlation between actual scores on the dependent variable and predicted scores based on the regression equation. Multiple R^2, the square of this, represents the proportion of variance predictable in the dependent variable from the regression equation a whole—by the entire set of variables collectively.

An ANOVA table for the regression equation is produced next; this represents a test of the null hypothesis that multiple R (and R^2) in the population equals zero. The variance of the dependent variable is partitioned into two sources: the part predictable from the regression equation ("Regression") and the part not predictable from the equation ("Residual," or error). In this example, the F-test is significant. As in simple regression, the sum of squares regression divided by the sum of squares total (i.e., regression plus residual) equals R^2.

The final section of the output provides the information needed to construct a least-squares regression (prediction) equation. The column labeled "B" lists the regression coefficients for each independent variable and for the "Constant" term. Thus, in this example, the least-squares prediction equation is:

Predicted *PartIndex* = −.889 + (.111)*Educ + (.006)*Age + (.003)*TObama + (−.003)*TMcCain

The values listed under "Beta" represent an alternative set of coefficients that would be used instead if all variables were first converted to Z-scores—if they were first standardized. Note that there is no value for "Constant" in this column: if all variables are in Z-score form, the Y-intercept is always zero. Thus, the prediction equation for predicting Z-scores on Y from Z-scores on the various predictors is:

$$\text{Predicted } Z_{\text{PARTINDEX}} = 0 + (.252)*Z_{\text{EDUC}} + (.084)*Z_{\text{AGE}} + (.072)*Z_{\text{TOBAMA}} + (-.071)*Z_{\text{TMCCAIN}}$$

These beta weights are in many ways more readily interpretable than the (nonstandardized) b weights, because they are all computed based on the same scale of standard deviation units. This is in contrast to the b coefficients, which are influenced by the scales of measurement of the different variables (e.g., *Age* and *Educ* are measured in years, whereas *TObama* and *TMcCain* are measured on a 100-point feeling thermometer scale). Examination of the beta coefficients suggests that *Educ* (*beta* = .252) is a moderately strong predictor, whereas the other three predictor variables are much weaker.

The last two columns report the results of the significance tests for the coefficients. The null hypotheses being tested are, in each case, that the b (and corresponding beta) coefficient in question equals zero in the population. In this case, all of the tests are significant at the .05 and .01 levels.

Stepwise Variable Selection

If you chose one of the stepwise methods of variable selection, the output will generally contain the results of several multiple regressions, in which each successive analysis adds or deletes one independent variable relative to the previous one. The final analysis reported is the one ultimately chosen by SPSS as the "best" equation as defined by that particular stepwise procedure.

Model Comparisons

If you specified a model comparison using the first procedure we discussed—by specifying the "full" three-predictor model and then removing two variables from it—the first two sections of your output will look like Figure 11.2. The first table is a reminder of what you asked SPSS to do, which is worth checking to make sure it is correct. In this case we requested that the variables *TMcCain, Educ, Age,* and *TObama* be entered in the first step ("Model" 1), and then *TMcCain, TObama,* and *Age* be removed from the equation in the second step ("Model" 2).

Regression

Variables Entered/Removed[c]

Model	Variables Entered	Variables Removed	Method
1	TMcCain, Educ, Age, TObama	.	Enter
2	.[a]	TMcCain, TObama, Age	Remove

a. All requested variables entered.
b. All requested variables removed.
c. Dependent Variable: PartIndex

Model Summary

Model	R	R Square	Adjusted R Square	Std. Error of the Estimate	Change Statistics				
					R Square Change	F Change	df1	df2	Sig. F Change
1	.266[a]	.071	.069	1.07096	.071	38.826	4	2042	.000
2	.226[b]	.051	.051	1.08131	-.019	14.231	3	2042	.000

a. Predictors: (Constant), TMcCain, Educ, Age, TObama
b. Predictors: (Constant), Educ

Figure 11.2 Output from Model Comparisons in Linear Regression analysis

The last part of the "Model Summary" contains the crucial test comparing the two models. The line for Model 1 gives R^2 (.071) for the four-predictor model and an F-test for the hypothesis that R^2 in the population equals zero. This test is significant and is identical to the one in Figure 11.1. The line for Model 2 then shows the *change* in R^2 (–.019) when the predictor variables *Age*, *TObama,* and *TMcCain* are removed. The F-test on this line tests the hypothesis that this change in R^2 equals zero in the population—the hypothesis that removing *Age, TObama,* and *TMcCain* has no effect on prediction. The significant result here—"F Change" = 314.231, df = 3 and 2042, "Sig. F Change" = .000—indicates that *Age, TObama,* and *TMcCain* do, in fact, collectively add to prediction above and beyond what can be predicted by *Educ* alone.

Had we used the alternative procedure, in which Model 1 included only one predictor and Model 2 added the two other predictors, the change in R^2 reported on the Model 2 line would have been a positive rather than a negative .019, but the corresponding F-test result would have been identical.

Conclusion

So, what do we conclude? Clearly, all independent variables are statistically significant predictors of political activity, and education is the strongest predictor of the four in terms of its influence on political activity. Interestingly enough, respondents who had higher levels of positive feelings about John McCain were less likely to participate in political activities. Thus, education, age, and feelings about Obama are statistically significant positive predictors of political activity, whereas feelings about McCain are a statistically significant negative (or "inverse") predictor of political activity.

Chapter 12

Logistic Regression

Sample Problem

In the sample problem in the previous chapter, two students conducted a multiple regression analysis at the request of their professor in order to determine the factors that predicted political activity. They used a scale of political activities (*PartIndex*) as their dependent variable. Notably, that scale was designed as a measure of political activities *other* than voting. Their professor has now asked them to conduct a similar predictive analysis, but this time they were asked to determine the factors that predicted whether someone did or did not vote in the 2008 presidential election. They decide to use the same four independent variables (*Educ*, *Age*, *TObama*, and *TMcCain*) that they used in their earlier analysis. The ANES includes a variable (*Vote2008*), which indicates whether respondents voted in the 2008 election. The codes for *Vote2008* are:

    1 = Voted
    0 = Did not vote

They decide to use this as their dependent variable.

  In the example in Chapter 11, multiple linear regression was the appropriate procedure for the students to use because the dependent variable (*PartIndex*) was a scale-level variable, representing a count of how many different kinds of activities someone had engaged in. In this new example, however, the dependent variable (*Vote2008*) is not a scale-level variable but rather a *binary*, *categorical* variable—a variable with only two possible values ("voted" and "did not vote"). Linear regression is not appropriate for such cases, so the students turn to a different kind of regression analysis.

Statistical Analysis

The appropriate statistical procedure to use here is a *logistic regression*, which is designed specifically to analyze the relationship(s) between independent variable(s) measured at the scale level and a binary-dependent variable (a dependent variable with only two categories). The two categories are typically coded as 0s and 1s.

Logistic regression is similar to linear regression in the important sense that the goal is to create an equation for predicting the dependent variable from one or more independent variables, in which a coefficient is computed for each of the independent variables, the magnitude of which reflects the degree to which it contributes to the prediction. As in linear regression, larger coefficients mean stronger prediction. The form of the desired equation looks much like a linear regression equation:

$$\text{Log odds (Category 1)} = a + b_1 * X_1 + b_2 * X_2 + b_3 * X_3 + b_4 * X_4$$

There are, however, at least two important differences. First, note that on the left side of the equation we are not computing "predicted scores" on the dependent variable, but rather "logged odds" of being in Category 1. Because the dependent variable has only two values, it does not make sense to talk about computing "predicted scores" because there are no scores between the values 0 and 1. Instead, we will now think about computing, for a given combination of X scores, the *odds* of being in Category 1 rather than Category 0 on the dependent variable. In the present case, we will want to predict the odds of one having voted (versus not) in the election. (We will explain why this is written as "log" odds below.) The second important difference is that the b coefficients in logistic regression are not interpretable as simple linear "slopes" as in multiple regression, but have a rather different meaning.

Mathematically, logistic regression computes an equation that, as noted above, predicts the *log odds* (sometimes written "logged odds") of being in Category 1. Because such logarithmic relationships are not at all intuitive, we will explain the results of logistic regression in the more easily understood terms of *odds ratios*, which tell us the percentage change in the odds of being in Category 1 of the dependent variable for each unit change in the independent variable. We will demonstrate in the *Output* section how to convert the coefficients produced by SPSS into a form that allows us to interpret a coefficient in these terms. For example, we will be able to say something like "each 1-year increase in education increases the odds of voting by 34%."

In our example, the dependent variable is *Vote2008*, which is already coded 1 and 0 in the ANES 2008 data set, and the independent variables are the scale variables *Age*, *Educ*, *TObama*, and *TMcCain*. The logistic regression analysis will tell us the odds of someone voting given a certain level of education, a certain age, and a certain rating of Obama and McCain. In terms of our specific example, the basic logistic regression model for this problem is:

$$\text{Log odds } (\textit{Voting}) = a + b_1 * (\textit{Educ}) + b_2 * (\textit{Age}) + b_3 * (\textit{TObama}) + b_4 * (\textit{TMcCain})$$

Running the Analysis in SPSS

Open SPSS and retrieve the ANES 2008 data file described in Chapter 3 (or, alternatively, one of the revised versions of it that you created in previous chapters). Then, be sure to set SPSS *options* per our instructions in Chapter 2.

Follow the procedure outlined in Chapter 11 on multiple regression, click on **Analyze** on the menu bar, and then choose **Regression**. From the resulting menu, this time choose **Binary Logistic . . . .** In the resulting dialog box (see Figure 12.1), move the variable **Vote2008** into the "Dependent" box and move the variables **Educ, Age, TObama,** and **TMcCain** into the "Covariates" box (with logistic regression, what we normally call dependent variables are referred to as covariates). Click on the **Options . . .** button and select "Iteration history" in the resulting dialog box. Click on **Continue** to close this dialog box, then on **OK** to run the analysis.

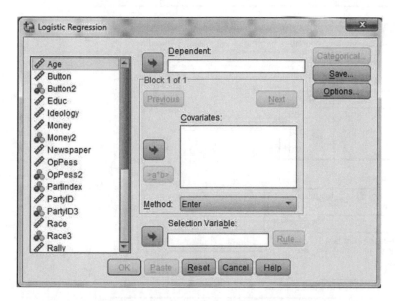

Figure 12.1 Main dialog box for Logistic Regression analysis

Output

The output produced by SPSS for the sample problem is shown in Figure 12.2. SPSS produces a lot of output, but we have only shown the few tables that we need to pay attention to here. Specifically, we have omitted the first six tables of output—everything up to "Block 1: Method = Enter"—as well as the table labeled "Classification Table." We will be examining the results starting at the end of the output and working backwards.

Logistic Regression

Iteration History[a,b,c,d]

Iteration		-2 Log likelihood	Coefficients				
			Constant	Educ	Age	TObama	TMcCain
Step 1	1	2019.627	-3.111	.202	.020	.006	.003
	2	1972.835	-4.875	.296	.031	.008	.005
	3	1971.245	-5.291	.318	.033	.009	.005
	4	1971.242	-5.309	.319	.034	.009	.005
	5	1971.242	-5.309	.319	.034	.009	.005

a. Method: Enter
b. Constant is included in the model.
c. Initial -2 Log Likelihood: 2235.569
d. Estimation terminated at iteration number 5 because parameter estimates changed by less than .001.

Omnibus Tests of Model Coefficients

		Chi-square	df	Sig.
Step 1	Step	264.327	4	.000
	Block	264.327	4	.000
	Model	264.327	4	.000

Model Summary

Step	-2 Log likelihood	Cox & Snell R Square	Nagelkerke R Square
1	1971.242[a]	.121	.182

a. Estimation terminated at iteration number 5 because parameter estimates changed by less than .001.

Variables in the Equation

		B	S.E.	Wald	df	Sig.	Exp(B)
Step 1[a]	Educ	.319	.025	163.436	1	.000	1.376
	Age	.034	.004	89.779	1	.000	1.034
	TObama	.009	.002	15.812	1	.000	1.009
	TMcCain	.005	.003	4.196	1	.041	1.005
	Constant	-5.309	.471	127.151	1	.000	.005

a. Variable(s) entered on step 1: Educ, Age, TObama, TMcCain.

Figure 12.2 Output from Logistic Regression analysis

Let us begin by going to the table titled "Variables in the Equation" at the very end of the output. As with linear regression analysis (Chapters 10 and 11), the column labeled "B" lists the regression coefficients for each independent variable and for the "Constant" term. Thus, if we insert the appropriate coefficients into our basic model equation, the logistic regression predictive equation would be:

Log odds (*Voting*) = −5.309 + (.319) * *Educ* + (.034) * *Age* + (.009) * *TObama* + (.005) * *TMcCain*

Each coefficient tells us the log odds of voting (remember, voting is coded 1 and not voting is coded 0, so our logistic regression analysis is predicting voting) while holding all other variables in the analysis constant. So, the coefficient for *Educ* tells us that, controlling for all other variables in the analysis, each additional year of education increases the logged odds of voting by .319. The coefficient for *Age* tells us that, controlling for all other variables in the analysis, each additional year of age increases the log odds of voting by .034, and so on with *TObama* and *TMcCain*. The column labeled "Sig." tells us the level of statistical significance of each coefficient. In this case, all but *TMcCain* are statistically significant at least at the .0005 (rounded to .000) level. *TMcCain* is (barely) significant at least at the .041 level (e.g., alpha = .05.).

As we noted earlier, however, speaking in terms of "log odds" is not practically useful to us. It would be more useful if we could speak in terms of *odds ratios*, which tells us the percentage change in the odds of the dependent variable for each unit change in the independent variable. The column labeled "Exp(B)" gives us this information, but before we can interpret it properly we need to carry out some simple subtraction and multiplication. For any particular predictor variable, subtract 1 from its corresponding Exp(*B*) value and then multiply by 100. The resulting number can then be discussed in terms of the percentage change in the odds of being in Category 1 (voting, in this case) on the dependent variable for each unit change in the independent variable. So, for *Educ* we would compute (1.034 − 1.000) × 100 = 34. Thus, each one year increase in education increases the odds of voting by 34%. That is a large number and clearly demonstrates the strong influence education has on voting. (To put the number in perspective, consider that a 100% increase would mean that the likelihood of voting *doubled*.)

The table titled "Model Summary" gives us two statistics (*Cox and Snell R-Square* and *Nagelkerke R-square*) that can be interpreted similarly to the R^2 from the linear regression analysis (as discussed in Chapters 10 and 11). The Cox and Snell statistic is a more conservative measure than the Nagelkerke statistics, but together they tell us something about the strength of our prediction of voting with the variables we have in our model. In this case, it is somewhere between 12.1% and 18.2%.

The tables titled "Iteration History" and "Omnibus Tests of Model Coefficients" give us the last bit of information we need, at least for now. Logistic regression uses a method called *maximum likelihood estimation* (MLE) to determine the most accurate estimates for the coefficients. To start with, MLE determines how much of the dependent variable can be predicted without knowing anything about the independent variables—a so-called "blind" model. This number is reported in footnote "c" below the "Iteration History" box as "Initial −2 Log Likelihood: 2235.569." Then, MLE adds the independent variables over and over again (in our case five times) to determine the model that is the best predictive fit. This best predictive fit for the model is the last number in the column labeled "−2 Log likelihood" in the "Iteration History" box. This number is 1971.270.

The difference between the "blind" model (the model that did not take into account any of the independent variables) and the best-fit model is 264.299 (that is, 2235.569 − 1971.270). This number turns out to be a chi-square statistic and, as reported in the box labeled "Omnibus Tests of Model Coefficients," it is statistically significant at least at the .0005 level (rounded to .000). The interpretation of this chi-square statistic is pretty straightforward. Our ability to predict voting is significantly improved by knowing *Age*, *Educ*, *TObama*, and *TMcCain* as compared with not knowing those independent variables.

Conclusion

So, what do we conclude? Clearly, all independent variables are statistically significant predictors of voting, and education is the strongest predictor of the four in terms of its predictive influence on voting; age is not far behind the predictive influence of education. Interestingly enough, how someone feels about Obama and McCain has a positive predictive influence on his or her voting, but have much less predictive influence than either age or education.

Chapter 13

One-Way Independent-Groups ANOVA

Sample Problem

In 2008, Barack Obama became the first African American major party presidential candidate in the history of the United States. Given this fact, Obama's race was an often-discussed topic among political commentators and the public. Many people were proud of Obama's achievements but this pride, some social commentators hypothesized, was especially high among African Americans and other racial and ethnic minorities because his achievements represented a broad social achievement for them.

In this chapter, we use *analysis of variance* (often referred to simply as *ANOVA*) to examine the question of how opinions about Obama, as measured by the *TObama* feeling-thermometer variable, differ across racial groups. To keep things simple, we will use the modified version of the ANES *Race* variable that we created in Chapter 5 (*Race3*), in which we reduced the large number of original race categories down to three: White, Black/African American, and "other minorities." There are many varieties of ANOVA, the simplest of which is appropriate for this situation in which we are comparing the means of *independent groups* (racial groups) with respect to scale-level variable. Although the mathematics will look very different, this kind of ANOVA has much in common with the *independent-samples t-test* discussed back in Chapter 8. That *t*-test was designed to compare the means of exactly two independent groups with respect to a scale-level variable. Although ANOVA can be used as well when there are only two groups (indeed it will produce results that are mathematically equivalent to those of the *t*-test), ANOVA has the advantage of being able to handle comparisons across more than two groups. It also provides a number of additional bells and whistles unavailable in *t*-tests, some of which we describe in this chapter.

Statistical Analysis

The ANES includes two variables that will allow us to examine this question: *Race3,* (created in Chapter 5) and *TObama*. In this problem, we are testing the null hypothesis that there is no difference in mean feeling-thermometer ratings for Barack Obama between Whites, African Americans, and other racial and ethnic minorities. That is:

$$H_O: \begin{array}{c} \text{Mean Obama} \\ \text{rating of} \\ \text{White} \end{array} = \begin{array}{c} \text{Mean Obama} \\ \text{rating of} \\ \text{African Americans} \end{array} = \begin{array}{c} \text{Mean Obama} \\ \text{rating of} \\ \text{other minorites} \end{array}$$

The test of this hypothesis, sometimes referred to as the "omnibus" null hypothesis, is conducted by computing an *F*-test. A statistically significant result means that we would reject this null hypothesis in favor of the alternative hypothesis that the three population means are not all equal—i.e., there is at least one inequality among them.

Post-Hoc Tests

Rejection of the "omnibus" null hypothesis in ANOVA tells us only that not all population means are equal: It does not indicate which means are significantly different from which others. One way to further examine mean differences is to use *post-hoc* or *a posteriori* multiple-comparison tests such as the *Student-Newman-Keuls* or *Tukey's HSD test*. In our example, we use Tukey's HSD tests to test for differences between all possible pairs of means.

Such tests are very much like simply running independent-groups *t*-tests to compare each pair of groups, that is, Whites versus African Americans, Whites versus other minorities, and African Americans versus other minorities. A problem with doing lots of "pairwise" *t*-tests, however, is that as you do more and more statistical tests on the same data, the odds keep increasing that you will "find" a significant result that you really should not. (Technically, this refers to the problem of an *inflated Type I error rate*.) The post-hoc tests discussed here are designed to take this into account, so that the overall rate of such errors does not get too large.

Planned Comparisons/Contrasts

Another approach to multiple comparisons in ANOVA is to test more specific hypotheses, which have formulated in advance, about which means (or combinations of means) differ from other means (or combinations of means). These tests are known as *planned comparisons*, *contrasts*, or *a priori* multiple-comparison tests. In our example, we will test two contrasts, each corresponding to a different null hypothesis. First, we want to test the null hypothesis that the mean for Whites is equal to the mean Obama rating of African Americans and other minorities. Mathematically:

$$H_O: \begin{array}{c} \text{Mean Obama} \\ \text{rating of} \\ \text{Whites} \end{array} = \frac{\begin{array}{c} \text{Mean Obama} \\ \text{rating of} \\ \text{African Americans} \end{array} + \begin{array}{c} \text{ratings of} \\ \text{other minorities} \end{array}}{2}$$

The appropriate contrast coefficients for this problem are:

−2 for Whites (*Race3* = 1)

1 for African Americans (*Race3* = 2)

1 for other minorities (*Race3* = 3)

Note that we could just as easily have reversed all the signs and used the coefficients 2, −1, and −1, respectively. (In either case, the coefficients for a given comparison must sum to zero.)

For the second contrast, we want to test the null hypothesis that the mean Obama rating for African Americans is equal to the mean Obama ratings for other minorities:

$$H_O: \begin{array}{c} \text{Mean Obama} \\ \text{rating of} \\ \text{African American} \end{array} = \begin{array}{c} \text{Mean Obama} \\ \text{rating of} \\ \text{other minorities} \end{array}$$

The appropriate contrast coefficients for this question are:

0 for Whites (*Race3* = 1)

1 for African Americans (*Race3* = 2)

−1 for other minorities (*Race3* = 3)

The coefficient of 0 for Whites explains that the mean of that group has no part to play in the analysis.

Note that this procedure divides up the original question about differences among three groups into two separate, logical parts. The omnibus *F*-test merely asks whether there is *any* variability among the means of three populations (vs. the null hypothesis that the population means are equal). Our two contrasts divide this question neatly and logically into two separate, independent (technically "orthogonal") questions: (1) Is there variability (i.e., a difference) between Whites and non-Whites? and (2) Is there variability (a difference) between the two categories of non-Whites? Two questions, two tests.

Running the Analysis in SPSS

Open SPSS and retrieve the (modified) data file that you created in Chapter 5 ("Making Comparisons"), which includes the *Race3* variable that we created in Chapter 5 but need again in this chapter. If you did not save that file, you will have to first go through the steps outlined in Chapter 5 to create *Race3* using the *Recode* command. Then, be sure to set SPSS *options* per our instructions in Chapter 2.

Click on **Analyze** on the menu bar, and then choose **Compare Means**. From the resulting menu, choose **One-Way ANOVA . . . .** This produces a dialog box that looks like Figure 13.1.

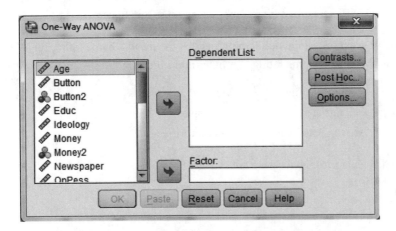

Figure 13.1 Main dialog box for One-Way ANOVA

This dialog box is very similar to that for the independent-samples *t*-test, as discussed in Chapter 8. In this dialog box, your list of variables appears in the box to the left, and you must (1) move one, or more, of your variables into the box labeled "Dependent List" to select your dependent variable(s) and (2) move *one* of your variables into the box labeled "Factor" to identify the groups to be compared (to select the independent variable).

First, click on **TObama** (the dependent variable in our example) in the left-hand box to select it; then click on the upper right-arrow pointing to the "Dependent List" box; **TObama** disappears from the left-hand box and reappears under "Dependent List." Next, click on **Race3** (the independent variable in our example) to select it, and then click on the right-arrow button pointing to the "Factor" box to move it there. The name *Race3* now appears under "Factor."

If you wish to have SPSS print out means and other descriptive statistics along with the results of the *F*-test—and, of course, you do!—there is still one more step. In the dialog box illustrated in Figure 13.1, click on **Options . . .** to bring up another dialog box. In this box, which is illustrated in Figure 13.2, click on the box under "Statistics," next to "Descriptive." Then click on **Continue** to return to the previous dialog box. If you wish to conduct only the "omnibus" ANOVA to test the hypothesis that all three population means are equal, you are done. Click on **OK** to execute the analysis. If, in addition, you wish to conduct tests of multiple comparisons, using either post-hoc tests or planned comparisons/contrasts, follow the instructions in the corresponding sections below before clicking on **OK**.

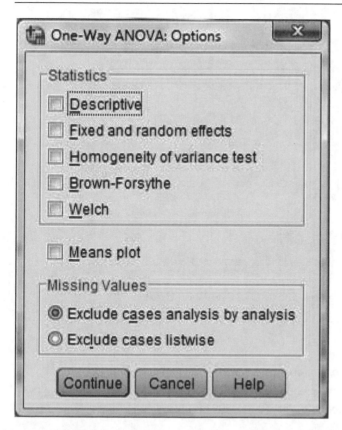

Figure 13.2 Dialog box for specifying Options in One-Way ANOVA

Post-Hoc Tests

To conduct post-hoc tests in SPSS, specify your variables, follow the steps above, and then click on the button labeled **Post Hoc . . .** at the right in the dialog box illustrated in Figure 13.1. This produces a new dialog box (see Figure 13.3) containing a list of available tests. For simple pairwise comparisons, the most commonly used tests are probably Student-Newman-Keuls (labeled "S-N-K") and the Tukey's HSD test (labeled simply "Tukey"). Simply click on the box(es) next to the test(s) you wish SPSS to calculate and print. Then click on **Continue** to return to the dialog box illustrated in Figure 13.1, and click on **OK** to run the analysis. To illustrate, the output produced by specifying Tukey's HSD test is reproduced later in this chapter.

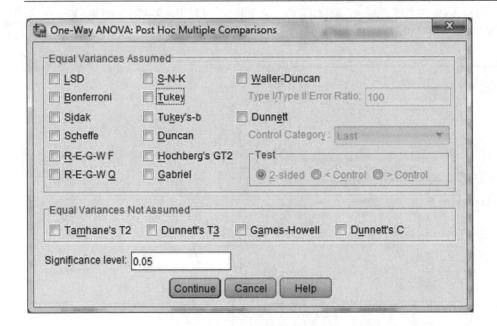

Figure 13.3 Dialog box for specifying post-hoc tests in One-Way ANOVA

Planned Comparisons/Contrasts

To conduct tests of planned comparisons or contrasts, specify your variables, and so on, as described previously, and then click on the button labeled **Contrasts . . .** at the right in the dialog box illustrated in Figure 13.1. This produces a new dialog box as illustrated in Figure 13.4.

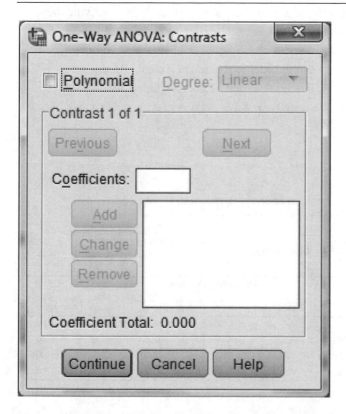

Figure 13.4 Dialog box for specifying Planned Comparisons/Contrasts in One-Way ANOVA

Specifying your contrast coefficients in this window can be a little tricky, but experiment a little and you will get the hang of it. For the first contrast in our example, we wish to use the coefficients –2, 1, and 1 (in that order) for *Race3* groups 1, 2, and 3. To specify these coefficients, click in the box to the right of "Coefficients" and type the number of the coefficient for the first (lowest-numbered) group, in this case **–2**. Now click on the button labeled **Add** to add this coefficient to your list of coefficients (which is displayed in the box to the right of the **Add** button). Now click in the "Coefficients" box again, and type the coefficient for the second group (in this example, type **1**), and then click on **Add**. Finally, click on the "Coefficients" box again, type **1** (the last coefficient), and click on **Add**. Your list of three coefficients now appears in the box to the right of the **Add** button: –2, 1, and 1, from top to bottom. If this is the only contrast you wish to test, click on **Continue** to return to the main One-Way ANOVA dialog box (Figure 13.1), and then click on **OK** to run the analysis.

In this example, however, we wish to test a second contrast as well. After specifying the coefficients for the first contrast as just described, click on **Next** to the right of the phrase "Contrast 1 of 1." This phrase now changes to "Contrast 2 of 2," which is what you will specify now. The box containing your previously entered coefficients is again blank. Repeat the procedure outlined above to enter the coefficients **0**, **1**, and **–1** in order. Once these have been entered, click on **Continue** to return to the main One-Way ANOVA dialog box, and then click on **OK** to run the analysis.

Output

The output produced by SPSS for the omnibus analysis is shown in Figure 13.5.

Oneway

Descriptives

TObama

	N	Mean	Std. Deviation	Std. Error	95% Confidence Interval for Mean		Minimum	Maximum
					Lower Bound	Upper Bound		
1.00	1302	63.70	27.632	.766	62.20	65.20	0	100
2.00	525	91.34	12.482	.545	90.27	92.41	40	100
3.00	254	76.14	23.149	1.452	73.28	79.00	0	100
Total	2081	72.19	26.863	.589	71.04	73.35	0	100

ANOVA

TObama

	Sum of Squares	df	Mean Square	F	Sig.
Between Groups	290345.171	2	145172.586	249.190	.000
Within Groups	1210595.326	2078	582.577		
Total	1500940.498	2080			

Figure 13.5 Output from One-Way ANOVA

The first part of the output displays a variety of descriptive statistics, including the means for each of the three groups. Consistent with the commentators' expectations, the mean for African Americans (91.34) is much higher than that for Whites (63.70), with others (76.14) intermediate between the other two groups.

The second part of the output presents the results of the ANOVA, including the crucial *F*-test for evaluating the null hypothesis of no differences among racial groups. Three sources of variability are listed: "Between Groups" (variability due to the treatment effect: differences between groups as a result of attachment style), "Within Groups" (variability reflecting random error), and "Total." For each, SPSS reports the sum of squares, degrees of freedom, and mean square (sum of squares divided by degrees of freedom).

The F ratio, calculated as the mean square between divided by the mean square within, is listed next in the table. The F ratio in this example equals 249.190, and its associated p-value ("Sig.") is reported as .000. As in previous examples, this does not mean that p is exactly equal to 0, but rather that the probability is $<.0005$ and has been rounded off to .000. Thus, we reject the null hypothesis and conclude that Whites, African Americans, and other racial and ethnic minorities differ with respect to the mean ratings they give Barack Obama.

Post-Hoc Tests

SPSS prints out the results of the Tukey's HSD tests in two different ways, as shown in Figure 13.6.

Post Hoc Tests

Multiple Comparisons

TObama
Tukey HSD

(I) Race3	(J) Race3	Mean Difference (I-J)	Std. Error	Sig.	95% Confidence Interval	
					Lower Bound	Upper Bound
1.00	2.00	-27.640*	1.248	.000	-30.57	-24.71
	3.00	-12.437*	1.656	.000	-16.32	-8.55
2.00	1.00	27.640*	1.248	.000	24.71	30.57
	3.00	15.203*	1.845	.000	10.88	19.53
3.00	1.00	12.437*	1.656	.000	8.55	16.32
	2.00	-15.203*	1.845	.000	-19.53	-10.88

*. The mean difference is significant at the 0.05 level.

Homogeneous Subsets

TObama

Tukey HSD[a,b]

Race3	N	Subset for alpha = 0.05		
		1	2	3
1.00	1302	63.70		
3.00	254		76.14	
2.00	525			91.34
Sig.		1.000	1.000	1.000

Means for groups in homogeneous subsets are displayed.

a. Uses Harmonic Mean Sample Size = 453.870.
b. The group sizes are unequal. The harmonic mean of the group sizes is used. Type I error levels are not guaranteed.

Figure 13.6 Output for post-hoc tests in One-Way ANOVA

Each of the six rows of the upper table represents a comparison of two groups; for example, the first row compares African Americans versus other. Actually, each comparison appears twice because the comparison of African Americans versus others (first row) is for all practical purposes the same as the comparison of White versus African American (third row), and so forth. In any case, for each pairwise comparison of interest, SPSS prints out the difference between the means (for example, −27.640 or −12.437 for African American versus other), along with a standard error, p-value ("Sig."), and confidence interval. In this example, African American and others are significantly different from each other (p is listed as .000, meaning it is <.0005 and rounded off) and White and others are significantly different from each other (again, p is reported as .000). Finally, White and African Americans are significantly different from each other (again, p is reported as .000).

The second part of the output presents this information in a different (and confusing) way, by identifying *homogeneous subsets* of means—that is, by showing sets of means that do not differ significantly from each other. In the left column, the groups are listed in order from that with the smallest mean (Whites in this case) to that with the largest mean (African American in this case). To the right are three columns listing the actual means, grouped into three subsets: Subset 1 contains White (mean = 63.70), subset 2 contains others (mean = 76.14), and subset 3 contains African Americans (mean = 91.34). This indicates that none of the three racial groups form a homogeneous subset whose means are not significantly different from one another. Each racial group is in a different subset, indicating that their means *do* differ significantly from each other. That is, the mean of each racial groups is significantly different from the mean of each other racial group.

Planned Comparisons/Contrasts

When contrasts or planned comparisons are requested, the output shown in Figure 13.7 is produced by SPSS in addition to the ANOVA results previously illustrated.

Contrast Coefficients

Contrast	Race3		
	1.00	2.00	3.00
1	-2	1	1
2	0	1	-1

Contrast Tests

		Contrast	Value of Contrast	Std. Error	t	df	Sig. (2-tailed)
TObama	Assume equal variances	1	40.08	2.279	17.587	2078	.000
		2	15.20	1.845	8.241	2078	.000
	Does not assume equal variances	1	40.08	2.180	18.385	1027.021	.000
		2	15.20	1.551	9.800	326.071	.000

Figure 13.7 Output for Planned Comparisons/Contrasts in One-Way ANOVA

SPSS produces a matrix of contrast coefficients (a reminder about which groups were assigned which coefficients for each test), followed by the significance tests for each contrast. Two different significance tests are provided for each contrast, labeled as "Assume equal variances" and "Does not assume equal variances," respectively. The more commonly used test is the one listed under "Assume equal variances." In this test, the error term for every contrast is based on the MS within from the omnibus ANOVA.

For each contrast, SPSS prints: (1) the value of the contrast itself, a linear combination of the contrast coefficients and sample means (labeled "Value of Contrast" in the output); (2) a standard error; (3) the observed t statistic; (4) the error degrees of freedom for the test; and (5) a two-tailed probability or p-value. In this example, the first contrast, which compares White with African American and others combined, is significant: $t = 17.587$ with 2078 degrees of freedom, $p = .000$ (that is, p is $<.0005$). The second contrast (African American vs. other) is also significant with $t = 8.241$ and $p = .000$.

Some formulas for calculating significance tests for contrasts by hand employ F-tests rather than t-tests. The t-tests computed by SPSS produce identical results to these tests: For each contrast, just square the observed t-value produced by SPSS to find the corresponding F-value.

Conclusion

So, what do we conclude? Can we reject our null hypothesis that there is no difference in mean feeling thermometer ratings for Barack Obama between Whites, African Americans, and other racial and ethnic minorities? Clearly, the answer is yes. But, does the analysis confirm the alternative (research) hypothesis advanced by social commentators that feelings toward Obama are especially high among African Americans and other racial and ethnic minorities as compared with white Americans? Yes, it appears that we can do that as well. It is also true, however, that African American participants rate Obama even more highly than do other racial minorities.

Chapter 14

Two-Way Independent Groups ANOVA

Sample Problem

A student who was home from school for a weekend got into a debate with his dad over the issue of gay and lesbian rights at dinner one night. His dad is opposed to expanding federal civil rights protections to gays and lesbians. The student believes that there is a generational difference—anyone he knows who is younger than 40 years of age has no problems with gays and lesbians, whereas most people he knows over 40 years of age are uncomfortable with gays and lesbians. Thus, he believes that this is the reason that older people oppose gay rights. His mother, however, states that she and most of her girlfriends have no problems with gay rights. She feels that it is mostly older men who are uncomfortable with gays and lesbians and subsequently oppose gay rights.

Thinking about the political science research methods class that he was in, the student decided to examine the issue further when he got back to school and had access to the ANES data set and SPSS. The ANES includes three variables that will allow for the examination of the question: *Age*, *Sex*, and *Tgaylesbian*. A two-way ANOVA will examine the hypotheses suggested by the student and his mom. First, do younger and older people (operationally defined, in this case, as 40-and-under vs. over 40) differ on average with respect to the negativity/positivity of their feelings about gays and lesbians? Secondly, do men and women differ, on average, with respect to such feelings? In ANOVA, these effects are referred to as the *main effects* of *Age* and *Sex*, respectively.

Of course, if we wanted to answer only these two questions, we could have simply done two separate independent-groups *t*-tests, as described back in Chapter 8, or two separate one-way ANOVAs, as described in Chapter 13. Either way, we could do one test to examine sex differences (male vs. female) in feelings about gays and lesbians, and a second to examine age differences (40-and-under vs. over-40). It turns out, although, that examining both effects simultaneously within the same analysis has the advantage of providing us, at no extra charge, with the answer to a third question. This question, concerning the *interaction* of age and sex, is one you might not even have thought about, but which is often extremely important. One way to describe the interaction in this case would be to ask however large the *average* sex difference (in attitudes) is, will this difference or effect be the same *size* among younger folks as it is among older folks? Alternatively, the question can be asked the other way around: however large the average age difference is (in attitudes), is this effect the same size among men as it is among women?

If you think about it a bit you can see why this third question is potentially very important. It is possible, for example, that *on average* women and men have very similar feelings about gays and lesbians. It is possible, however, that this is because among young individuals, men have more positive attitudes than women, but among older individuals, it is the women who have more positive attitudes. When you lump the age groups together it looks as if sex has no effect, but this is because the sex difference goes in one direction among younger respondents, and the opposite direction among older respondents, and so when you simply lump the older and younger respondents together the two effects cancel each other out. Alternatively, you might find a relatively small main (average) effect of sex, but in this two-way analysis discover that this is because in one age group there is a huge sex difference, but in the other age group the sex difference is very small—so, when you lump them together you find something in-between. Analyzing the effects of sex and age simultaneously in a two-way ANOVA can provide potentially important insights that would be completely invisible if the independent variables were examined only one-at-a-time.

Statistical Analysis

In statistical terms, as noted above, the questions about these three effects are referred to respectively as the *main effect* of age, the *main effect* of sex, and the *interaction* of age × sex. For each, the null hypothesis is that the particular effect does *not* exist in the population, and the alternative hypothesis is that it does exist (to some nonzero degree). As in the simpler one-way ANOVA discussed in Chapter 13, each null hypothesis is evaluated by an *F*-test, and a sufficiently small *p*-value (i.e., <.05 or .01) means that the size of the particular effect observed in the sample is larger than could be reasonably explain by chance (random sampling error).

Running the Analysis in SPSS

Open SPSS and retrieve the ANES 2008 data file described in Chapter 3 (or, alternatively, one of the revised versions of it that you created in previous chapters). Then, be sure to set SPSS *options* per our instructions in Chapter 2. Because we want specifically to compare respondents who are 40 years old and younger to those who are over 40 years old, we will have to first recode the ANES 2008 age variable into a new variable distinguishing these two specific categories. To do so, follow the procedure outlined in Chapter 2 to recode the variable *Age* into a new variable called *Age2* representing the two specific age categories (under- vs. over-40) that we need to answer our question. For this new age variable, we want to recode the original *Age* values 17 through 40 into a new *Age2* code of 1 (to represent respondents 40 years of age and younger), and recode *Age* values 41 through 90 into a new *Age2* code of 2 (to represent all respondents older than 40 years of age). This new variable will now serve, along with *Sex*, as an independent variable in a two-way ANOVA.

Click on **Analyze** on the menu bar. Next, choose **General Linear Model** from the pull-down menu, and then choose **Univariate**. This produces a dialog box that looks like Figure 14.1.

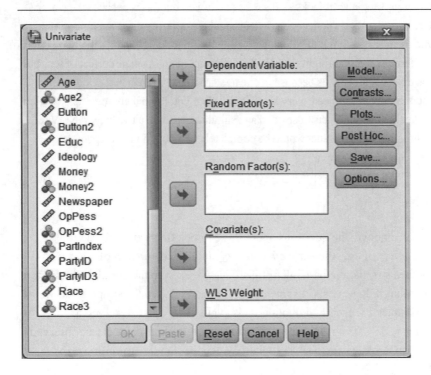

Figure 14.1 Main dialog box for Two-Way Independent-Groups ANOVA

This dialog box is very similar to that for the independent-samples *t*-test and the one-way ANOVA, as discussed in Chapters 8 and 13. In this dialog box, your list of variables appears in the box to the left, and you must (1) move one of the variables into the box labeled "Dependent Variable" to select your dependent variable and (2) move one or more (in this example, two) of your variables into the box labeled "Fixed Factor(s)" to identify the independent variable(s). So, click on **Tgaylesbian** (the dependent variable in our example) in the left-hand box to select it; then click on the upper right-arrow pointing to the "Dependent Variable" box; **Tgaylesbian** disappears from the left-hand box and reappears under "Dependent Variable." Next, click on **Age2** (our first independent variable) to select it, then click on the right-arrow button pointing to the "Fixed Factor(s)" box to move it there. Now repeat these steps to select the second independent variable (factor), **Sex**. Click on **Sex** in the left-hand box, and then on the arrow pointing to the "Fixed Factor(s)" box to move it there.

If you wish to have SPSS print out means and standard deviations for your six cells in addition to the results of the *F*-test—and of course you do!—click on the button labeled **Options**, which produces a new dialog box as illustrated in Figure 14.2. Click on the box to the left of the phrase "Descriptive statistics." This tells SPSS to print out your cell means and standard deviations. As part of the "Descriptive Statistics" output, SPSS will print out the *weighted* marginal means for your independent variables. Because our *n*s, however, are not all equal we wish to see *unweighted* marginal means. To do so, click on the word **Age2** in the upper-left corner of the dialog box (see Figure 14.2), in the section labeled "Estimated Marginal Means," to highlight the word, and then click on the arrow in the upper-center of the box so that **Age2** appears in the right-hand list. Then move **Sex** in the same way. "Estimated marginal means" is SPSS's name for what we are calling *unweighted* marginal means.

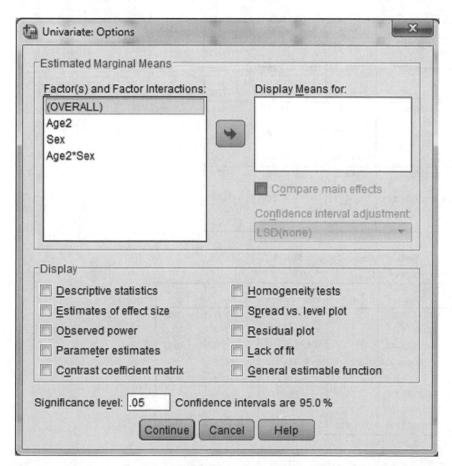

Figure 14.2 Dialog box for specifying options in Two-Way Independent Groups ANOVA

Click on **Continue** to return to the dialog box illustrated in Figure 14.1, and then click on **OK** to run the analysis.

Output

If you requested descriptive statistics, part of your output will look like Figure 14.3. (The section of output labeled "Descriptive Statistics" will not appear if you did not request these statistics.)

Univariate Analysis of Variance

Descriptive Statistics

Dependent Variable: Tgaylesbian

Age2	Sex	Mean	Std. Deviation	N
1.00	1 1. Male respondent selected	48.28	26.962	349
	2 2. Female respondent selected	59.38	25.235	448
	Total	54.52	26.567	797
2.00	1 1. Male respondent selected	40.42	27.570	524
	2 2. Female respondent selected	51.23	28.189	702
	Total	46.61	28.423	1226
Total	1 1. Male respondent selected	43.56	27.583	873
	2 2. Female respondent selected	54.41	27.355	1150
	Total	49.73	27.968	2023

Tests of Between-Subjects Effects

Dependent Variable: Tgaylesbian

Source	Type III Sum of Squares	df	Mean Square	F	Sig.
Corrected Model	89422.663[a]	3	29807.554	40.331	.000
Intercept	4712153.489	1	4712153.489	6375.769	.000
Age2	30355.975	1	30355.975	41.073	.000
Sex	56965.299	1	56965.299	77.077	.000
Age2 * Sex	10.284	1	10.284	.014	.906
Error	1492186.717	2019	739.072		
Total	6584060.000	2023			
Corrected Total	1581609.380	2022			

a. R Squared = .057 (Adjusted R Squared = .055)

Figure 14.3 Output from Two-Way Independent-Groups ANOVA

The cell means, standard deviations, and sample sizes (N) of the dependent variable *time* are produced for each combination of levels of the independent variables. The arrangement in which the means are printed is a bit awkward, however, and makes it difficult to "see" the main effects. These means might better be arranged, in accordance with the two-way nature of the design, as follows:

Cell Means for Male and Female by Age

Age	Young	Old
Male	48.28	40.42
Female	59.38	51.23

The cell means within the table were taken directly from the "Descriptive Statistics" section of Figure 14.3. The so-called *weighted* marginal means can also be found there, in the various rows labeled "Total." For example, the (weighted) marginal mean for young (40 and under) respondents, collapsing across sex, is 54.52; for older respondents (41 and over) this marginal mean is 46.61. In Figure 14.3, this value appears in the first row labeled "Total" in the "Descriptive Statistics" section. Collapsing across age groups, the (weighted) marginal means for males and females are 43.56 and 54.41, respectively, as shown in the bottom section of the "Descriptive Statistics" table.

Because our ns are not all equal, however, we typically wish to see *unweighted* marginal means instead. Also known as *equally weighted* means, these are computed by finding the mean of the means across the relevant cells, such that each cell contributes equally to the marginal mean despite the fact that the various cell means are based on different ns. These unweighted marginal means, appear separately at the end of the output in an "Estimated Marginal Means" section (Figure 14.4). "Estimated marginal means" is the term SPSS uses for unweighted means. These unweighted marginal means are somewhat different than the weighted marginal means discussed earlier. For younger versus older respondents, respectively, these equal 53.827 and 45.829; the male and female (unweighted) marginal means are 44.349 and 55.307.

Estimated Marginal Means

1. Age2

Dependent Variable:Tgaylesbian

Age2	Mean	Std. Error	95% Confidence Interval	
			Lower Bound	Upper Bound
1.00	53.827	.970	51.924	55.731
2.00	45.829	.785	44.290	47.368

2. Respondent: gender

Dependent Variable:Tgaylesbian

Respondent: gender	Mean	Std. Error	95% Confidence Interval	
			Lower Bound	Upper Bound
1 1. Male respondent selected	44.349	.939	42.508	46.191
2 2. Female respondent selected	55.307	.822	53.695	56.919

Figure 14.4 Output for Unweighted marginal means in Two-Way Independent-Groups ANOVA

In between the "Descriptive Statistics" and "Estimated Marginal Means" sections of the output are the results of the significance tests, labeled "Tests of Between-Subjects Effects" (see bottom half of Figure 14.3). The line labeled "Error" refers to the "error term" used in all of the F-tests. In this example, $SS_{error} = 1492186.717$, $df_{error} = 2019$, and MS_{error} (found by dividing SS_{error} by df_{error}) = 739.072. This last value is used as the denominator in the F ratios for testing the main effects and interaction.

The three sources of variability of primary interest are: (1) *Age2*, which refers to the main effect of age; (2) *Sex*, which refers to the main effect of sex; and (3) *Age2 * Sex*, which refers to the interaction of the two independent variables. For each, the sums of squares ("Type III Sum of Squares"), degrees of freedom ("df"), and mean square are reported, along with the F ratios and p-values ("Sig.") for the significance tests. Each F is calculated as the ratio of the mean square for a particular effect divided by the MS_{error}, and is associated with a "Sig." or p-value. On the line labeled *Age2*, we can see that the main effect of *Age2*, with $F = 41.073$ and p-value of .000 (i.e., <.0005), is clearly significant at either the .05 or .01 level. The line labeled *Sex*, with $F = 77.077$ and p-value of .000, indicates that the main effect of *Sex* is also significant. According to the line labeled *Age2* × *Sex*, however, the interaction between the variables ($F = .014$, $p = .906$) is clearly not significant.

Conclusion

It turns out that both the student and his mom were right. We can reject our null hypotheses with respect to the main effects of both age and sex. Feelings toward gays and lesbians are on average significantly more positive (or, less negative) among people aged 40 and under than among people over 40, and also are significantly more positive (less negative) on average among women than among men. The absence of a significant interaction indicates that the size of the age effect is about the same for both men and women or, stated conversely (but equally correctly), the size of the gender effect is about the same among both younger and older respondents. In other words, the two effects are simply *additive*. This is consistent with the mom's additional perception that it "was mostly older men who were uncomfortable with gays and lesbians": Men on average have more negative attitudes, and older people in general have more negative attitudes, so the additive effect results in older men having the most negative attitudes of all.

Using Syntax in SPSS

Using the Syntax Method: Why?

As we mentioned in Chapter 1, using SPSS back in the "old days" required users to type out commands (*syntax*) to specify their analyses, long before it was possible to use a mouse or other device to point-and-click one's way through menus of options. Today, we have the option of using SPSS in this "point-and-click" way, and so it is not necessary for most purposes to learn any of this command language. It is still there, although, behind the scenes. When you choose various program options by pointing-and-clicking, the program actually translates your actions into SPSS command language internally and then executes the commands. This command language is what is printed at the very beginning of your output whenever you run an analysis in SPSS.

The old-fashioned "syntax method," in which users actually type in commands to specify their analysis, is still available in SPSS as an alternative way of specifying analyses. But, you might well ask, why bother? Why take the time to learn what is essentially a new computer language if you do not have to?

Generally speaking, we have no argument with this and agree that the point-and-click method is a much simpler way to use SPSS for many (or even most) purposes. There are situations, however, in which learning how to use the syntax method has certain advantages, or is even necessary. Most of these have to do with the realities of doing "real" research, in contrast to running a handful of analyses for a homework assignment. When conducting research for publication in professional journals, for example, it is common to run many, many analyses on the data before selecting the ones that eventually are reported. In addition, these data analyses are often done over long periods of time. It is not unusual to return to a data set many months after you last used it, in which case you may well have forgotten much of what you did the first time. Finally, it is not uncommon for the data set itself to change over time (e.g., because you identify and fix errors, or new cases are added to the data) in which case it becomes necessary to go back and repeat numerous analyses you did previously. In all of these situations, writing (and saving) command syntax is often much easier and more efficient than repeatedly pointing-and-clicking your way through menus. In light of these kinds of situations, there are several reasons why it will be worthwhile, and perhaps even necessary, to learn how to use syntax, at least if you plan to get involved in research in the future.

First, syntax is very useful when you have reason to perform numerous variations of some specific task. For example, you might have a large number of variables that you want to recode in the same way, which can be accomplished by writing and executing one or two lines of simple syntax. Or, you might want to repeat the (almost) same analysis many times with minor variations (e.g., running the same analysis on numerous dependent variables), in which case it is easy to write the syntax for the analysis once, and then edit it (e.g., change that one variable name) for each new variation.

Second, once you have created a syntax file containing your commands, you can save that file to your computer for future reference. This is a simple way of keeping a kind of log of what you have done so far, which can be especially useful for keeping track of how you created new variables, recoded old ones, and so forth. (These are the kinds of things that are easy to forget a week or month after you have done such things.)

Third, having saved the syntax from analyses you did previously is a life-saver if you make any changes to your data, and then have to go back and replicate all of the analyses you did on the now-obsolete data set. Rather than having to point-and-click your way through numerous analyses (not to mention having to remember exactly what you had done the first time) you can simply retrieve your saved syntax file and execute any or all of your original analyses exactly as they were specified previously.

Finally, it turns out that for certain kinds of analyses, you simply *must* use syntax because particular options or specifications that you require are not available via menus and dialog boxes. All of the (relatively simple) kinds of analysis covered in this book can be done by pointing-and-clicking, but as your analyses become more advanced it is just a matter of time before you confront this situation.

Assuming that we have now successfully persuaded you that it is worth learning a little syntax, we explain how to do so in the remainder of this appendix. In the first section below, we outline the basic procedure for writing, executing, and saving syntax commands. Then, we provide the syntax for each of the analyses covered in this book, chapter by chapter. Running these commands should produce exactly the same results as you found when you did them previously using the point-and-click method.

Using the Syntax Method: How?

To use the Syntax Method, you need a *Syntax Editor* in which to type and edit SPSS program commands ("syntax") to specify any desired transformation or analysis. To open the Syntax Editor (1) click on **File** on the menu bar, then (2) click on **New** in the resulting pull-down menu, and finally (3) click on **Syntax** in the resulting submenu. The Syntax Editor now appears in the foreground, as illustrated in Figure A.1. (If necessary, you may expand it to fill the screen by using the *maximize* button.)

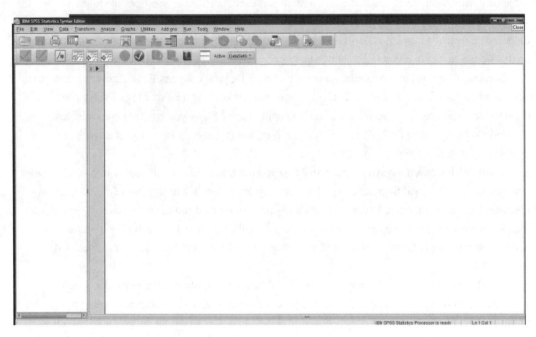

Figure A.1 The Syntax Editor window

At this point, the Syntax Editor window is blank, and a cursor appears in the upper-left corner of the main section (right-hand side) of the window. If you begin typing, what you type will appear in the window at the point where the cursor is located. As you will see, this window operates very much like a (very simple) word-processing program, and you can use the *Delete* (or *DEL*) key, the *Insert* (or *INS*) key, the *Backspace* key, and so forth to edit your commands and correct your errors. Later in this chapter, we explain exactly what to type into this window to specify each analysis covered in this book.

In recent years, SPSS has made some significant modifications to the Syntax Editor to make learning and using syntax easier. You will notice that as you begin to type a command, drop-down menus will sometimes pop up to guide you. Once you have typed a few letters, SPSS tries to guess what it is you want to do and provides a list of commands that begin with the letters you typed. You can simply ignore this and keep typing if you know what you are doing and do not need the help, or you use the menu as a reference to confirm that you do in fact know what you are doing. Or (and this seems somewhat ironic to us) you can use your mouse to point-and-click on the menu option you want, in which case SPSS will "type" it for you. In addition, you will see that SPSS will change the colors of words you have typed at various times, distinguishing (for example) commands that are complete and ready to run versus those that require additional information. You can make use of these features to whatever extent you find useful.

The narrow window on the left side of the screen is designed to serve as a kind of table of contents for your syntax. You do not have to do anything over here, as SPSS will automatically add items to this section as you type commands in the main window. Having a table of contents can be useful if you have a large number of syntax commands, especially if there are more lines of syntax than you can see at one time in the main window. Clicking on any item on the left side will take you to that particular command on the right side.

Executing ("Running") the Analysis

Once your commands have been typed into the Syntax Editor, you need to tell SPSS to "execute" or "run" them—that is, to actually carry out the instructions you have written. To do so, click on **Run** on the tool bar at the top of the screen to produce a menu of options including (among others) **All** and **Selection**. As you might expect, **All** will execute all of the commands currently in the Syntax Editor, starting at the beginning. **Selection**, in contrast, run only those commands that have been first selected by highlighting a set of commands (accomplished by clicking-and-dragging the mouse, as you would do in a word-processing program). If no set of commands has been selected in this way, clicking on **Selection** will simply execute whichever command currently contains the cursor. Click on one of these options and SPSS will leap into action.

Saving the Syntax File

Given that many of the reasons for using syntax involve keeping it around for future use or reference, you will want to save the contents of the syntax window to a file. The procedure for doing this is similar to that for saving data files, as described previously in Chapter 1. From within the Syntax Editor, click on **File** on the menu bar, and then choose **Save** from the resulting drop-down menu. (Alternatively, choose **Save as** to save the file under a different name than its current name.) Use the buttons at the top of the resulting dialog box to navigate to the folder in which you want to save the file, and then type the name you wish to give the file in the box next to "File Name." By default, SPSS will save the file in the proper format, and add *.sps* (SPSS's name for syntax files) to the end of whatever name you provide.

Syntax for Problems in this Book

In the remainder of this appendix, we provide the syntax commands for running each of the analyses described in Chapters 4 through 14 of this book. If you type these commands exactly as written here, you should get exactly the same results as you did by pointing-and-clicking.

Chapter 4: Frequency Distributions and Descriptive Statistics

```
FREQUENCIES
/VARIABLES = SEX IDEOLOGY TPALIN
/STATISTICS = ALL.
```

Histograms:

```
FREQUENCIES /VARIABLES = TPALIN /HISTOGRAM.
```

Bar Graphs:

```
FREQUENCIES /VARIABLES = IDEOLOGY /BARCHART.
```

Chapter 5: Making Comparisons and Controlled Comparisons

Data Transformations:

```
RECODE PARTYID (1=1) (2=3) (3=2) INTO PARTYID3.
RECODE RACE (1=1) (2=2) (3 THRU 7 = 3) INTO RACE3.
```

Comparisons:

```
CROSSTABS
/TABLES=PARTYID3 BY SEX
/FORMAT=AVALUE TABLES
/CELLS=COUNT COLUMN
```

Controlled Comparisons:

```
CROSSTABS
/TABLES=PARTYID3 BY SEX BY RACE3
/FORMAT=AVALUE TABLES
/CELLS=COUNT COLUMN
```

Chapter 6: Chi-Square Test of Independence

Data Transformations:

```
RECODE OPPESS (1=1) (2=3) (3=2) INTO OPPESS2.
```

Analysis:

CROSSTABS /TABLES = IDEOLOGY BY OPPESS2
/CELLS = COUNT EXPECTED ROW COLUMN
/STATISTICS = CHISQ GAMMA D.

Chapter 7: One-Sample t-Test

T-TEST
/TESTVAL = 2
/VARIABLES = Newspaper.

Chapter 8: Independent-Samples t-Test

T-TEST
/GROUPS = SEX (1, 2)
/VARIABLES = TPALIN.

Chapter 9: Correlations

Data Transformations:

RECODE TALK RALLY BUTTON WORK MONEY (1=1) (5=0) INTO
        TALK2 RALLY2 BUTTON2 WORK2 MONEY2.
COMPUTE PARTINDEX = TALK2 + RALLY2 + BUTTON2 + WORK2 +
        MONEY2.

Analysis:

CORRELATIONS /VARIABLES = AGE EDUC PARTINDEX.

Including means and standard deviations:

CORRELATIONS /VARIABLES = AGE EDUC PARTINDEX
/STATISTICS = DESCRIPTIVES.

Kendall's tau-b coefficients:

NONPAR CORR /VARIABLES = AGE EDUC PARTINDEX
/PRINT = KENDALL.

Spearman's rho coefficients:

NONPAR CORR /VARIABLES = AGE EDUC PARTINDEX
/PRINT = SPEARMAN.

Chapter 10: Simple Linear Regression

```
REGRESSION /DESCRIPTIVES
/DEPENDENT = PARTINDEX
/METHOD = ENTER EDUC.
```

Scatterplot Graphs:

```
GRAPH /SCATTERPLOT (BIVAR) = EDUC WITH PARTINDEX.
```

Chapter 11: Multiple Regression

```
REGRESSION
/VARIABLES = PARTINDEX EDUC AGE TOBAMA TMCCAIN
/DESCRIPTIVES
/DEPENDENT = PARTINDEX
/METHOD = ENTER EDUC AGE TOBAMA TMCCAIN.
```

Model Comparisons:

```
REGRESSION /STATISTICS COEFF OUTS R ANOVA CHANGE
/DEPENDENT = PARTINDEX
/METHOD = ENTER EDUC AGE TOBAMA TMCCAIN
/METHOD = REMOVE SUPPORT EDUC.
```

...or

```
REGRESSION /STATISTICS COEFF OUTS R ANOVA CHANGE
/DEPENDENT = PARTINDEX
/METHOD = ENTER EDUC
/METHOD = ENTER AGE TOBAMA TMCCAIN.
```

Chapter 12: Logistic Regression

```
LOGISTIC REGRESSION /VARIABLES = VOTE2008
/METHOD = ENTER EDUC AGE TOBAMA TMCCAIN
/PRINT=ITER(1).
```

Chapter 13: One-Way Independent Groups ANOVA

```
ONEWAY /VARIABLES = TOBAMA BY RACE3
/STATISTICS = DESCRIPTIVES.
```

Post-Hoc Tests:

ONEWAY /VARIABLES = TOBAMA BY RACE3
/STATISTICS = DESCRIPTIVES
/RANGES = TUKEY.
Planned Comparisons/Contrasts:

ONEWAY /VARIABLES TOBAMA BY RACE3
/CONTRAST –2 1 1
/CONTRAST 0 1 –1.

Chapter 14: Two-Way Independent-Groups ANOVA

Data Transformations:

RECODE AGE (17 THRU 40 = 1) (41 THRU 90 = 2) INTO AGE2.

Analysis:

GLM TGAYLESBIAN BY AGE2 SEX
/PRINT = DESCRIPTIVE.
/EMMEANS = TABLES (AGE2)
/EMMEANS = TABLES (SEX)